PRAISE
FOR WOVEN

"Judi is one of the kindest, most courageous, and most selfless people I've had the pleasure of knowing. From the moment we met, I knew Judi's heart yearned to help others and put their needs before her own. Nothing could be more evident than her tireless support of JT Townsend and his family, and ultimately, the creation of her foundation, Champions for Hope. Judi's loving nature, strong work ethic, and tireless positive energy have led her to help numerous people throughout her community. Despite her health battle, she has never let that impact her ability to give back. She is an inspiration to her community and the state. The world would be a better place if there were more people like Judi Zitiello. I'm one of the lucky ones who have the honor of calling her my friend."

– Florida First Lady, Casey DeSantis

"There is great beauty in the baring of one's soul journey and by doing so, a blessing is always revealed."

- Jean Trebek, American Entrepreneur, Philanthropist and Blogger

"Inspiration if often found in mysterious ways. Judi Zitiellos' sharp wit, captivating storytelling and deep compassion come through the pages as she tells her remarkable story. Her gift of seeing the blessings that come, even from hardship, is inspirational and shows how God can turn even the most heartbreaking events into good."

- Fred Funk, PGA Tour Professional

woven

A Single Thread Led to My True Purpose

by Judith Zitiello

ISBN: 978-1-66788-838-5

"Therefore, we do not lose heart. Though outwardly we are wasting away yet inwardly we are being renewed day by day. For our light and momentary troubles are achieving for us an eternal glory that far outweighs them all. So, we fix our eyes not on what is seen, but on what is unseen. since what is seen is temporary, but what is unseen is eternal."

2 Corinthians 4:16-18 NIV

This book is dedicated to my husband, Tommy, whom I now call my Joseph. Thank you for rescuing me from myself and believing I was the person God wanted me to be. Then, helping me to be her.

Prologue

IT SEEMS PRETENTIOUS TO WRITE about ones' life, so full of yourself. From the time I was a teenager I dreamed of writing a fictional biography about a girl with an extraordinarily colorful and fascinating life. Unlike my sad and often embarrassing one.

As decades passed, surprisingly, my life seemed to take on some color. In fact, it turned out far better than where I was headed.

My siblings and I often question how we turned out so level-headed and responsible considering the way we grew up.

I compare my life to a hand-sewn quilt or tapestry, full of tone and texture, beautiful to behold. But a true seamstress knows the most remarkable part is the underside, the side that touches the body. Where the threads are knotted to secure the buttons and colorful stitching.

My mother taught me to embroider when I was around ten. She made certain the backside of the cloth was neat and flawless. The threads had to be taut, and the knot ends cut very short, but not too short so they didn't ravel. She guided me just as her mother had her.

Today, like a worn-out quilt, my underside is far from flawless. My knots have grown softer, the buttons are gone, my broken threads have fallen away, and I am left as a shredded piece of cuddly, soft material that I pray will hold together until my final day.

Life has not been comfy and cozy. Two failed marriages and an early life of turmoil. Storms still brew and the winds still blow. Time has allowed me to discover how to accept my life and all that comes along with it, the roses and the thorns.

And truthfully, the later part of my life is the richest. Navigating through the dark times and reaching near the rainbow's end, I have come to understand so many important life lessons. I have grown and blossomed, thanks to many difficult mistakes and a treasure that was there all along that I didn't see.

My parents were good examples of what I didn't want my life to be like. This is precisely why I didn't want to write my true memoir. I was reluctant to openly share that they made me feel unloved and unworthy. It was many years before I realized my parents did the best they could with the history they had to draw from. I don't blame them or anyone else anymore for my shortcomings. I tried to figure out what love language Mom and Dad were speaking to me. That question became too time-consuming to answer. I had more important things to ponder.

One strong underlying thread ran through my life. From the earliest memory I have, I felt it. There was a needle that pointed me in the right direction. I didn't always follow that point, but I felt it nonetheless. God was leading me through the peaks and valleys, protecting and refining me with every success and failure, urging me to find my true purpose.

He had a job for me to do, and He wasn't going to give up on me like many had. He was going to follow me right through eternity.

This is not my story. This is His story, a testament to faith, love, grace, and belief.

1

Judith Ann

1949

S HE TRACED THE SIGN OF the cross slowly on my small forehead baptizing me with the anointing oil. I was six weeks old. My grandmother was not going to risk my soul going to purgatory where all babies who were not baptized in the name of the Lord went. And she didn't stop there. She would hold my tiny hand and pull me alongside her as we walked several blocks from her apartment to mass. Before we reached the heavy wooden doors, she would open her pocketbook and remove a dainty handkerchief and place it on my head. I would step carefully so the hankie didn't slip. When we found our pew, she would reach back into her purse for the small pouch that held the felt and ribbon scapular with the picture of the Sacred Heart of Jesus and another of the Blessed Mother holding baby Jesus, she would place it over my head so it would hang one depiction over my heart the other on my back. My mother's mother was going to protect her grandchildren regardless.

Decades later, this action would become an important piece of my history and erase one of my most egregious sources of guilt, guilt that haunted me each Sunday as I bowed and stepped in front of the priest and accepted the sacrament of the Holy Eucharist.

My parents were married on Mom's seventeenth birthday at the side altar of the Catholic Church, while Dad's parents waited in the car. Dad and his family, immigrants from England, were Anglican Lutheran. They would never be seen stepping foot inside a Catholic Church. So, they waited in the car till the ceremony was complete and the happy couple emerged as Mr. and Mrs.

It was 1941, and my dad was heading off the join the fight. The Germans dropped bombs over Britain during the Blitz of World War II. Salisbury, Leicester, and surrounding villages had been targeted, where his grandparents, aunts, and cousins lived. His mother would spend her days on the settee next to the radio listening to the war coverage as she wept and wrung her hands. He felt compelled to join the fight to protect the family he had never met across the seas.

When Dad, the oldest of two sons, was just six weeks old, he and his parents set forth from England across the Atlantic to Canada, considered a Dominion under the crown of the United Kingdom. The Canadian government offered free land to all Brits who would leave their motherland to begin a new life there. Other relatives had sent word that it was a wonderful place, full of opportunity. It was enticing for my grandfather, a young man from a huge and wealthy family to embark on this adventure.

Arriving in Quebec on May 22, 1921, wife and baby in tow, they lived a short while with family who had taken advantage of the free land opportunity in Montreal. However, Grandmother didn't like Canada and wanted to see America. So, they picked up once again and traveled into the United States to Detroit, Michigan through Windsor, Ontario.

They heard of the abundance of jobs with the auto plants there. Once they determined this was going to be their home, they purchased a great brick house with two floors, a finished basement, and a detached garage in a small suburb, Royal Oak, a quiet neighborhood just north of Detroit, to raise their family.

"Pop," my grandpa on my dad's side, was a watchmaker by trade. The auto industry had taken hold there and jobs were plentiful. The Grand Trunk Railroad crossed southern Michigan to Chicago, Illinois, and beyond, carrying assembled automobiles. Switchmen were required along the tracks to change the rails at specific times to send the trains to different destinations. Pocket watches needed synchronizing. Pop opened "Green's Jewelers and Watch Repair," a small shop just north of Detroit in Ferndale, a few blocks from home. My grandmother worked alongside him selling delicate English bone china teacups and saucers and restringing pearls for lady customers, while he worked at his repair table fixing and timing watches. It was a successful part-time business to supplement his hourly income from Ford Motor Company.

My mother's family lived a very different lifestyle. Grandpa was a Detroit city fireman. He was a stocky man with bulging muscles. A cook at the fire hall, he was known to be able to lift a wooden fire ladder with one hand. Mom was the second daughter of three girls and a boy. Midwestern winters were long and cold. They lived in the city during the school year but when school let out and summertime came, they pulled a small camper north to Pontiac Lake. Grandpa would work three days on and three days off. He would join them at the lake to fish and enjoy the humid Michigan summers. Grandpa's mother was there to help with the kids. Mom told me she wore her swimming suit most of the summer. She held fond memories of their summers on the lake.

The fall of her thirteenth year, Mom met my dad, a friend of her older sister's boyfriend. She accompanied her sister to a lunch box social at the church. Four years older, Dad sat playing the piano and singing "Stardust" the same song Frank Sinatra sang when Harry James introduced him in his earliest days as a singer at the Roseland Ballroom in New York. Dad asked her to come sit next to him on the piano bench. She said she fell in love that day with the handsome guy with a twinkle in his eye and a wave in his hair.

Naturalization paperwork was lax when Dad came through Canada to Michigan in the early 1920s. When he went to sign up with the US Air Force in early 1941, they told him he would have to go back to Canada and join the Royal Canadian Air Force. He did and completed officer's school where he graduated as a bombardier. Paperwork would not thwart his resolve. He was off to the European theatre to defend England for his family.

Mom lived with "Pop" and Amy, my grandparents, while Dad was overseas. She worked as an elevator operator in the Penobscot Building downtown Detroit. Shortly after their wedding, she discovered she was pregnant. My sister was born the next spring to my Grandparents' delight … their first granddaughter.

Dad's parents were socialites, members of the Masonic Temple and the Eastern Star. It was a very different life for this young mother, but she tried her best to show her appreciation by cleaning and ironing and keeping Amy's hair looking freshly coiffed. They loved her baby, and she was thankful for that.

It was common for families to rent out a room for supplemental income during the war, and my grandparents were no different. They rented the upstairs to an Englishman. My Grandfather, "Pop" as we lovingly called him, had met Harold at the Ford Motor Company. Harold joined meals and family celebrations. He drove my Grandparents around town for grocery shopping and errands. Grandma Amy made their lunches each working day, filling large thermos bottles with hot coffee or tea and preparing tasty sandwiches wrapped in waxed paper saved from her bread loaves. Harold was fun to be around and loved my sister as if she were his own. We never considered him less than a member of the family, and he always handed a quarter to any child who came to visit.

Mother decided to go to cosmetology school while Dad was away. As her skills improved, Amy and her friends would ask her to style their hair in pin curls and occasionally give them a box permanent. She would give them facials with new products by Merle Norman or do their nails and apply their makeup. She felt like she was helping to repay their generosity toward her and her baby girl.

When Dad was granted furlough, the family would pack up and drive through the Windsor Tunnel and into Canada to see him. It didn't happen often, so they made the trip whenever they could. He was happy to see the baby and his young wife as well as his parents.

On one of the visits, Mom became pregnant. When she shared the good news, my grandmother arranged to "take care of it." She had one child to care for while her husband was away. How could she possibly take care of another? This decision would torment my mother forever. The strong Catholic values her parents had instilled were shaken to the core. This was a venial sin she believed she could never be forgiven for.

When World War II ended, May 8th, 1945, Dad returned to pick up life where he had left off and entered engineering school at Lawrence Tech. He graduated with his journeyman's card. He took a job as a tool and die maker at the Ford Motor Company. They rented a small bungalow just a few blocks from Dad's parents. Finally, his little family was together under one roof. He asked Mom to quit cosmetology school. "No wife of mine will go off to work." They were very happy, and within two years, Mom was pregnant again. She and her sister-in-law were due just a month apart.

She visited her doctor who said things were moving along nicely and it wouldn't be long before she would be holding the baby in her arms. That night she went into labor, and they rushed to the hospital. It was a difficult labor and when the small baby girl arrived, she was lifeless. My mother was convinced that God had punished her for having an abortion. She grieved for weeks.

Dad took all of the nursery things and new cuddly baby clothes to his brother and sister-in-law so she wouldn't be reminded.

Soon after, Dad was offered a position with a large heavy equipment company that sold, repaired, and rented heavy equipment being used to build the new highway I-75 that would stretch from Northern Michigan all the way south to Key West. He would become Sales and Service Manager and later Operations Manager over the Southfield and Jackson locations. His job required him to travel the state, wining and dining his road construction customers.

A few years passed and finally she was pregnant again. This time, a baby girl was born and thankfully perfect. I arrived in the beginning of a beautiful orange and crisp Michigan fall weighing seven pounds and twenty-one inches long.

2

Her Name Is "Judy"

1953

M Y SISTER STAYED OVERNIGHT WITH the grandparents frequently. They loved their first grandchild and spoiled her with pretty dresses and toys. Now that she was not working, Mom could focus on her newborn full time. She loved her babies.

Mom knew right away what she would name me. My sister had an imaginary friend named Judy. "Judy, Judy, Judy" … Cary Grant said to Rita Hayworth in the 1939 hit *Only Angels Have Wings*, making the name popular for the time.

However, this Judy was nothing like her imaginary friend. In fact, she tore pages from her books and pulled the clothes off her dolls. This little sister was certainly not the best friend she knew as Judy.

Mom's parents had purchased a cabin in West Branch in the middle of the state. They truly loved the pine-scented woods and fishing on the beautiful Clear Lake. It was a great place for our aunts, uncles, and cousins to gather with its knotty-pine walls, large stone fireplace, and big galley kitchen. Grandpa would prepare mounds of bacon and pancakes on the griddle with real maple syrup. Grandma Kathy would pick strawberries fresh from her garden. I remember the taste of those strawberries warm from the summer sun. We had a huge sandbox and swings Grandpa had made from trees he had cut down, painted green, then nailed together. Grandma Kathy would sit on the metal glider in the yard and watch us play. It was a wonderful place to escape the summer heat of the city.

Shortly after my parents bought a house in Royal Oak, my grandparents left West Branch and moved in temporarily with us. Grandpa was very sick and had been diagnosed with cancer of the pancreas. They pressed into one another and prayed for the best.

The only hope for him was an experimental drug made from snake venom. He had dropped about eighty pounds and looked nothing like the big, burly fireman we all loved. He died a few months later at fifty-five.

Dad's parents also had a cottage on Upper Straits Lake in West Bloomfield Township. It belonged to Harold, the man who lived upstairs in my dad's parents' house we grew up in. It was a small cottage on a hill overlooking the lake. Lilies of the Valley grew wild as ground cover along the hill.

They would pack up the car with all the supplies for the weekend and off to the cottage they would head. When we arrived and opened the door entering the kitchen, there was a familiar odor—musty and damp. Pop would check the rooms for any traces of wildlife because once a squirrel had come in through the fireplace and hid acorns in Pop's slippers.

The long set of wooden steps leading down to the dock and the water were a challenge for us, but we loved playing on the shore in our bathing suits.

Pop had a slick wooden outboard motorboat tied up to our dock and loved fishing. He would return from his day on the lake with a stringer of fresh fish and begin fileting his catch immediately.

We all loved fish and chips. Grandma Amy would fry potato wedges in a huge fryer filled with oil. She would let us help salt them when they turned golden brown. She would dump the hot fries into a paper grocery bag with salt and we would shake them for a minute or two while singing and dancing across the floor. Flour would float through the small kitchen as she breaded the fish and added them to the fryer. We ate the fresh fried fish with malt vinegar and tartar sauce. It was a delicious family favorite.

When I was four, Mom and Dad decided to move to the suburbs. They found a small ranch-style home in West Bloomfield. It was great to be able to live near the lakes Mom always told us about and we had grown to love. Her sisters, brother, and families followed shortly afterward.

The brick house with a carport was very mid-century. The black teak lamps with white fiberglass oval shades they bought were considered modern. A rose-colored textured sofa with black fringe in a very contemporary curved shape with blonde spindle legs sat next to the lamp in the living room. The slick tile floors were cool in the summer heat.

Mom loved to garden, so it wasn't long before she had beautiful flowers, lilac and forsythia bushes growing tall in the yard. I can still smell the freshly mown grass as she pushed the red Briggs and Stratton gas-powered mower beneath my bedroom window early in the morning before the heat set in. She enjoyed doing this, and besides, Dad was on the road and not around to keep up the trimming, mowing, and weeding.

She made friends with the lady next door who had a large family. But she stuck close to her sisters and their husbands who dropped by daily to sit at the dining room table and chat before they went to work on the night shift.

My sister, Sherrie, now in her teens began acting out. Mom had no car of her own. She had to rely on her brother and sisters for transportation. Many nights I was scooped up from my bed by my uncle and put in the car while the two of them searched my sister's usual hideouts. The night usually ended in a screaming match when they found her. I would cry myself to sleep wondering what was going to happen next.

3

Grandmother Kathy—"Lady Katie"

I LOVED TO VISIT MY GRANDMOTHER, Mom's mother, at her small apartment in downtown Detroit. She wore a full-length mink coat, mink hat, and knit scarf to shield her from the blistering winter Detroit air as she walked to the bus stops that would carry her to bingo or for a visit out to the suburbs. She would travel from her children's homes, house to house until her welcome was worn out, then back home to her tiny place.

She loved to play cards and sing. She would tune the black-and-white TV to *The Lawrence Welk Show* and sway around the living room to *"Red Roses for a Blue Lady."* She loved to bake and cook and made delicious lemon meringue pies and chop-suey from scratch with fresh vegetables and pork. The house smelled wonderful when she would visit. She was such fun to be around. And it was good company for us all because Dad seemed never to be around much.

My cousins on my mom's side lived on a lake just a few miles from us and attended a Catholic school. We spent a lot of time together, growing up. When I asked why I couldn't go to school with them, Mom would explain that Dad had said when I was old enough, I could decide what religion I wanted to follow. I was far too young to understand the explanation. Whenever I slept over, I would go to church with them, and I loved it.

The church adjacent to the school they attended was beautiful, with stained glass windows along rows of blonde wooden pews leading to the altar and the huge wooden cross where Jesus hung, his head down and blood dripping from his hands, feet, and side. Grandmother explained the story of Jesus and told me how much He loved me.

The bright morning sun would stream through the windows, casting beautiful rainbow colors on the congregation. The organist would play a familiar song while we joined in with the choir, softly singing the familiar words. The altar servers were dressed in white gowns over red robes. They lit the candles and attended the priest throughout the mass. The priest wore a colored robe with a white lace cassock and a beautiful colored vestment draped over his shoulders. He stood behind the marble altar and led the mass. At one point he whispered prayers then turned walking over to a table behind him. On the table sat an ornate gold cabinet. He would open the two vertical doors and carefully remove a gold chalice covered with a white cloth. It was magical. He would pray holding the host up to the heavens and everyone kneeled in silence. I would watch attentively at the mystical ceremony. Slowly the congregants in each pew stood in turn and walked past the statue of the Virgin Mary with downcast eyes dressed in a beautiful blue robe toward the priest single file at the steps to the altar to receive the Eucharist, everyone but me.

Each mass was the same. The prayers were always the same. And I began to repeat them with the others. It was beautiful and I felt safe.

Grandmother Kathy knew the importance of giving this small amount of time to God and made certain I did too.

Mom or Dad never came with us.

4

Young Life With "Bim and Aud"

WHILE HE WASN'T VERY TALL, Dad was big on looks. He had dark hair combed back with Vaseline hair-cream. There was a wave just over the left side of his forehead. He was always freshly shaven and smelled of Old Spice, his clothes perfectly pressed. He was successful, stylish, and came from class, and it showed.

Mom was too. She had high cheekbones and sparkling blue eyes. She took great pride in her appearance, fixing her thick, dark hair and keeping her nails done. Most days she wore a sleeveless white shirt, dark pedal pushers, and white Keds, her hair pulled up with a scarf. But, on special occasions, she wore tall heels and a dark taffeta skirt that stood straight out when she twirled. I thought she was the most beautiful woman in the world.

She kept the house spotless and Dad's work wardrobe perfectly pressed and ready to be packed in his suitcase at a moment's notice. Certainly, this was my mother's love language, acts of service. I am certain she believed she was the perfect wife, mother, and housekeeper.

Dinners were another thing. She seldom cooked for us because she figured what was the sense? Dad was not coming home. So, she made a cocktail and relaxed and listened to her favorite 78's on the walnut hi-fi. We were in bed and asleep by 7 PM after a hot dog and canned beans or spaghetti from a can.

Mom's outbursts became more frequent, and sometimes violent. She continued to have a difficult time controlling my sister. She would scream through the house chasing after her with the rubber hose she used to clean the fish tank, flying in her upstretched arm. Beating my sister was a regular occurrence. The more my sister would act out, the more frequent the beatings. Dad was never around when my sister acted out. This was another source of guilt she could lay on him when he finally returned home. It terrified me.

Today I wonder what really was going on between my mother and my sister. Was she seeking Mom's attention or was Mother just plain drunk and taking it out on my sister that her husband was never home? I was too young to understand this complex adult situation. All I knew was life at home was mostly tumultuous.

Each fall, Grandma Amy, Dad's Mother, took me back-to-school shopping at JL Hudson. We would search for a dress for each day of the week, new shoes, socks, and panties, slips, and my favorite thing of all, a winter coat. After my new wardrobe was purchased, we ate lunch at the department store dining room. I would order the chicken potpie and she the Waldorf salad. I felt special spending the day with her. It was all about me and I loved it.

A few days before school started each year came a family ritual. Mom and her sisters would gather us all at our house where Mom would give us box permanents. The kitchen would be filled with a strong ammonia smell. My cousins and I joined the ritual when we were around eight years old. As Mom twisted my fine poker straight blonde hair covered in thin paper strips around and around the plastic curler, it pulled and hurt. She would ooh and ah as she rinsed the foul solution out and pulled the curlers and wet papers from my curls dropping them into the sink. A quick sudsing with Breck shampoo and conditioner left the bouncy little curls a stark contrast from the poker straight bangs she left untouched. My cousins and I tolerated it, but we still had fun as we organized and showed off our new school clothes and supplies ready for the school year ahead.

While I truly didn't know anything different, I believed this was life as everyone knew it.

5

A Norman Rockwell Picture?

JUST AFTER THANKSGIVING ONE YEAR, my sister was taken to the doctor. Mom's fifteen-year-old curvaceous daughter was pregnant. She delivered a beautiful baby girl just six weeks later. In 1956, this was an unspeakable situation.

Christmas was approaching. One of Dad's co-workers wanted to drop by the house to bring Dad a gift bottle of his favorite scotch, *Cutty Sark*. My sister was told to stay in the bedroom. I could feel the shame of it all. I was seven years old.

The nineteen-year-old baby daddy had enlisted in the US Marine Corp just a few months before. He was called home at Christmas, and they married because it was the right thing to do. He was so handsome in his uniform. I tagged along to the movie theatre to see *Blue Hawaii* and I remember thinking he resembled Elvis Presley. My niece was born just three weeks later.

It was fun to have a baby in the house. She giggled and cooed and was just adorable. I hurried home from school each day to play with my real baby-doll.

My sister and I have always been very close. She was eight years older than me, but about twenty years more mature. My sister attended my school functions when Mom did not. She was there for orchestra concerts when I played the violin on stage. She came to an award banquet where I received a good citizen award. She listened to my problems over the years and counseled me when I needed it. I spent nights at her house often. She would make popcorn and we would play games or watch a movie. I loved being around Sherrie, her husband Bill, and the kids.

Dad was gone most of the time traveling the state with his job. He claimed he had to entertain the customers purchasing expensive pieces of road construction equipment. Mom would call his office and they would tell her he was in town. She would get neatly dressed, fix her hair, and apply her makeup, then prepare dinner. She would have a scotch and water while she waited for him. She would tell me to ride my bike to the highway and wait for his red and white 1960 Oldsmobile Dynamic 88' convertible to come around the corner. I would wait. And wait. Dad never came. When dark fell, I would ride my bike back home disappointed. Mom would be listening to the hi-fi with a glass in her hand. I would eat my dinner alone and go to bed.

Occasionally, to get out of the house, Mom would ride her bike with me hanging on to her waist about four miles to her sister's house. Aunt Lil and her family lived on Cass Lake, one of the largest lakes in West Bloomfield Township. My cousins and our mothers would pile into their small boat for a day on the lake. We would water-ski or swim while the sisters drank ice-cold beer, they had trailed in a fish net behind the boat. I can still smell the gasoline from the motor mixed with the fresh water from the lake.

Mornings before school I tried to keep as quiet as possible. Mom was seldom up before I left but always home when I arrived. I would find her out in the yard tending her beautiful flowers or ironing and enjoying a cold beer. She never left the house because she had no transportation. She took pleasure in telling Dad on the phone we had no food, and she had no way to get any, he needed to come home.

A new Lutheran Church with a great youth group program was opening at the top of my street. I agreed to go along with some friends one week and I was hooked. I loved the activities, bowling and horseback riding and snow-skiing in the winter. There was always hot chocolate and music and plenty of cute boys.

The youth group teacher was the father of one of the most popular boys in middle school. I loved how he spoke about God and family. Sometimes he would even tear up. I was completely touched. He told me about God's promise to love me unconditionally. He told me there was not one thing in the world I could do that God would not forgive. He would love me no matter what. I felt such a peace when I left the church. I couldn't wait to get back.

The Lutheran service wasn't much different from the Catholic mass I was accustomed to, and it wasn't long before they were baptizing me and preparing me for confirmation. I needed a sponsor. Being Lutheran, Dad agreed. I put on a special dress and felt proud as we drove the car up to the church sitting next to my handsome Dad. We sat in the second row with the rest of the newest church members. When we began to sing "The Old Rugged Cross" I noticed Dad was crying. I didn't know what to think, but we made it through the service. It was official. I was now a member of the church. My friends were elated and so was I. Dad and I drove home in silence. Each Sunday, rain, shine, sleet, or snow, I would walk to that church. But my family never went another day with me.

It seemed as if we were always waiting for Dad to come home. Every day Mom expected today would be the day. It was almost as if we were not complete without Dad in the picture.

A picture. That was how our life could be described. Like a Norman Rockwell picture complete with the perfect house, beautiful flower garden, perfectly dressed children. Mom refused to believe our life wasn't perfect like that picture, and nobody else suspected it wasn't perfect either.

6

"Zoo Bisou Bisou..."

Like a storyline from a *Mad Men* episode, Dad (Don Draper) met a redheaded grieving widow over scotch and a pack or two of Winston's at a bar he would frequent near his office. She was casting and he was trolling. It wasn't long before he was spending his travel time at her apartment just a few miles from work.

Dad and his lady, I use the term very roughly, quickly established a comfortable routine. Dad stayed with her when he was in town, except for Saturday night. He would try to make it home to our house at least one weekday night and each weekend. But, as the years passed, his nights at home lessened even further.

Dad's family, my grandparents, and his brother, knew this woman and accepted her, including her at their house for parties. They may have considered her a better choice for their son than my mother. It was all so dysfunctional.

We seldom visited Dad's brother and my cousins on the "other side" of the family. Later I realized Mom must have felt betrayed knowing they knew the truth.

Christmas Eve was spent at Grandma Amy and Pop's every year as far back as I can remember. We would dress up in special holiday outfits Mom had shopped for, Dad would come home from work early, and we would head back into the city the car filled with presents, where my cousins would be waiting for us to arrive.

There were always family friends at the party most of them from England. Grandpa Pop had a long wooden bar in his finished basement. Bottles and bottles of gin, whisky, and scotch lined the knotty pine shelves. The fridge held bottles of Miller High-Life, Seven Up, Vernors Ginger Ale, and Squirt. On the bar were bowls of salty pretzels and nuts. As the night progressed everyone who gathered around the bar would join in singing Christmas carols, then old English songs. Inevitably young Uncle Cal would be persuaded to sing "Oh Danny Boy" followed by tearful smiles as they reminisced about holidays long past.

The children were ordered to sleep upstairs until midnight. The clock would strike twelve and we would run down the stairs to open the presents Santa had delivered for us. It was always such fun.

As I grew older, it seemed we were waiting longer and longer at home for Dad to come home from work to drive us the thirty-minute car ride to Grandma Amy and Pop's house. I would be bathed and dressed early, and Mom would sit on the sofa and drink a cocktail while we played Christmas songs on the hi-fi, and stared at the beautiful lights of the Christmas tree, brimming with wrapped gifts underneath. I would lie on the floor or sit in a chair nearby guessing what was in each gift labeled for me.

Occasionally I would run to the window to check out a car coming up the snow-covered street to see if it was Dad. It was always someone else. When he finally did reach home, Mom was in no shape to go to the party and neither was Dad.

Dad would say he had been shopping for last-minute gifts. To his credit he would come in with boxes wrapped in beautiful paper and bows. I am sure he felt this would make up for his tardiness. Let me just say, those last few years were not pretty. Christmas became an anxious time, a sharp contrast to the joy we once shared.

Mom must have thought if she just had another baby, he would come home to her. So, at thirty-five she was pregnant, unheard of for the times. Dad had just met his mistress and was falling in love. Mother and Dad's relationship was slowly unraveling. Mom was going to make it so he had to stay no matter what.

On May 15, 1960, when I was ten, my brother was born. I remember the day he came home from the hospital. Grandma Kathy, dressed in her white nurse's uniform, was there to help Mom. Grandma loved babies and was experienced in caring for them as a part-time night nurse. This time it was for her very own daughter and grandchild. The baby was such a joy. He was beautiful with his chubby cheeks. I fell instantly in love again with my real-life baby doll.

But, as soon as school let out, just two weeks after my brother was born, my grandmother Kathy and I were on a Greyhound Bus headed south to Beaufort, South Carolina, where my sister and her husband Bill were stationed with the Marine Corp. She was due to deliver her second baby in August and we were going to help her.

Why couldn't I stay home with my new little brother? I was heartbroken. Three months seemed an eternity at ten years old and I longed for home and that sweet baby boy. We didn't return until a few days before school started in September.

At least I was with my sister. Her daughter was now four years old and adorable. Grandma Kathy helped with the little one and prepared great meals for us. She loved to bake, and the house was often filled with the sweet aroma of cinnamon and apples, a warm welcome.

This military assignment at Parris Island completed my brother-in-law's last tour of duty. He would leave the Marine Corp on September 1, 1960. Pressure was on for my sister to deliver the baby before he was released. Thankfully, and with the help of long walks and castor oil, her baby boy was welcomed on August 28th, just under the wire and perfect. We packed up, cleaned the base housing till it sparkled, and moved everyone and everything back to Michigan just in time for me to start fifth grade.

7

If You Don't Come Home, You Don't Love Me

ONE NIGHT IN MY EARLY teens, Mom came into my room to awaken me. She was staggering as she pulled me by the arm down the hall to the kitchen where the black wall phone hung. She had a phone bill in her hand.

"I'll dial the number and you ask to speak to your father."

After dialing the phone number she read from the phone bill, she handed me the receiver. A woman's groggy voice answered hello. I asked for my dad. Several seconds passed and Dad finally came to the phone. I told him exactly what my mom told me to tell him,

"*If you don't come home, it means you don't love me*"

He seemed dazed. I repeated what Mom had told me to say while we both cried.

He never came home.

When Dad was at home it was a shit show. Uncles and aunts, cousins, and often my sister, brother-in-law, and kids would come over for an outdoor barbecue and a dip in the redwood above-ground pool they had installed in the backyard. It was fun for my little brother to be around his cousins, nieces, and nephew. However, the adults would drink all day and by nightfall they would be hammered. Conversation would heat up and I would lay on the floor by the door to my bedroom listening to them talk, doors slamming as some left the house, wondering what would happen next.

Mom was very close to her sisters and brother. In fact, they were a huge support for my mother. They loved her unconditionally, and I guess she would draw on that love to maintain some sort of sanity. I know she didn't share everything with them because the picture she had painted and she thought they believed, would be destroyed. Dad was perfect in her eyes and everyone else's, or so she thought. She protected him, or maybe she was just embarrassed to admit the awful truth—he had fallen for another woman, and she couldn't keep him from her.

When we moved to the suburbs, her sisters and brother soon followed. It was fun to play with my cousins. We were always outside. We lived on the water, so we fished, swam, and boated regularly.

One of my cousins was just a couple of years older than me and we were very close. We shared our deepest secrets. Her father was harshly strict and would drink several bottles of wine when he got home from his calls as a television repairman. He drove a large box truck with "Conrad's TV Repair" painted on each side. He would rock in his gooseneck rocker next to the television while we played nearby. As night fell, he would pick up his pace rocking faster, and the dark green wine bottles would line up next to the rocker. If we made a noise or bothered him in any way, he would move his arm across his chest as if he was going to backhand us, glaring. He terrified me. If I spent the night, we would have to stay quiet in our beds until Uncle got up.

At home my little brother was adorable, and I loved him like crazy. He had white hair and huge blue eyes and thin little lips—a sweet boy. Mom would pull him in his red wagon over to her sister's house just around the corner. Mom's sister had a daughter just a year older than my brother. The cousins would play while the sisters rocked in the glider in the yard talking and enjoying a beer. Mom loved her baby boy too.

My little brother was bathed and put to bed early each night. I turned in after homework was finished. The evening belonged to Mother.

Mom would not allow me to spend the night at my girlfriends'. She was going to keep an eye on me, so I didn't follow down the same path as my sister. I longed to go to my friends' houses where their parents were fun to be around! But, when it came time to go to bed, I had to be home. My friends didn't understand.

It was a time of girls exchanging sweaters and skirts and Beatle records. I could do none of that; so many rules for a girl looking for acceptance. I was in middle school and boys were suddenly very interesting to me. I started "going steady," which really didn't mean more than we were an item, sending notes back and forth or talking on my princess phone for hours under the sheets. That summer my friends started to meet at the beach in a group and go to dances at the Sylvan Lake Rec Center. I was growing up and I wanted to be a part of the "in" crowd.

Mom kept a tight leash on me and would report our misbehaviors to Dad when he finally returned home. This made more tension for everyone. Dad tried to be the peacemaker when he would grace us with his presence. Mom always threw out "I'm going to tell your father." And she did just that. Dad would look at us in disappointment. That was worse than any beating she could give us. All we ever wanted was Dad's love and acceptance. To disappoint him was the worst thing we could do.

I remember looking at my mother and thinking she was beautiful. I loved her so much. She loved her babies. She bonded with each of us when we were newborns. But her love seemed to drift as we grew more challenging and older. I didn't feel her love any longer. I was developing a voice I longed to share with her, but I didn't want to start any turmoil.

As we grew and became independent her desire to parent faded. She seemed disconnected from us, in her own little world that consisted of her home, her siblings, her scotch and her obsession with keeping that picture perfect. All we had to draw from was the picture she had painted of what a normal family was like. Yet, our reality was far from normal.

She was obedient to her husband, just as she had been taught. She assumed incorrectly she had no value other than that of housekeeper, mother, and occasionally when he needed her, a wife.

It was a difficult time in my life, but I could dream.

8

A Future?

MOM DIDN'T ENCOURAGE US OR even ask us our plans for a future. As a girl she had never thought about going to college, so why would we think we were so special? Trade schools were a better option. They would get you into the work force much quicker. Besides, it cost money to attend college, money they didn't have. She stressed that at eighteen we would be out of the house and on our own.

Dad, on the other hand, a college graduate, encouraged us to take college prep courses in high school. But he never planned a way to pay for college. He was never around to discuss our goals or plans or let us feel he could make a way to make college happen.

At fifteen, I took a job at Peoples Food Market. I volunteered to work for free if they would train me. The manager, a sweet Italian, Frank, agreed. It was a good excuse to be out of the house during the school week. And my boyfriend just happened to be a bagboy. He could pick me up in his 59' Pontiac and drive me to and from work. It was my first real job.

When I approached my mom to sign a work permit because of my age, she refused to believe I had already gotten a job. I sold her on the benefits of having my own spending money and gaining experience.

"But how will you get there?" she asked.

I wasn't allowed to date until I was sixteen.

"I could grab a ride with this nice boy," I said.

The perfect solution to that problem, how could Mom refuse? She went along with my plan. I felt like I had walked out from under a big black cloud and into the sunlight.

Freedom was invigorating. I could not wait to get out of the house. Plus, I really liked this boy. Or was he just my ticket out of the house? He was a year ahead of me and graduated high school in 1966 and immediately joined the Army. He was going off the fight for his country. Truth later revealed he was avoiding the draft and a certain deployment to Viet Nam. But by enlisting it was suggested he would not see combat.

My senior year was unremarkable. Mentally done with school and my sweetheart away at boot camp, most of my friends had given up on calling me. I had completely thrown myself into my relationship with my future husband. I had accumulated so many credits towards my college prep degree Dad insisted on, that I was easily accepted into a co-op work program. I went to school just one or two hours in the morning. I worked every day and all weekend long at the supermarket. Church was missed so I could work and get double time pay. The independence I felt was great. I didn't think I needed to go to college. After all, I was going to be getting married and live the life of a military wife. What was the sense? I was seventeen years old, but hey, so was my mom when she got married.

While I wasn't going to church anymore, I still said my rote prayers. It was all I knew. Mom had taught me the Lord's Prayer and Hail Mary, but she never told me I could have a conversation with my Heavenly Father. In fact, she told me not to ask for anything from Him because He was very busy with miracles and listening to everyone else. Not a strong foundation for a girl who needed divine guidance.

Decisions I made were based on escape from my dysfunctional family life and survival. Not once did I consult God or anyone, not even my sister whom I trusted and loved deeply. I would figure this out myself. Mom had taught me to be independent. I had a plan in the works, and I would see to it that I carried it out.

9

Marriage and a Career

THE VIETNAM CONFLICT HAD BEGUN. Many of my classmates were anxious they would be drafted. Several of my friends enlisted and the news of casualties of upperclassmen began to circulate. It was such a turbulent time.

The city of Detroit had its own "Haight Ashbury," Plum Street. On weekends my cousin and I would cruise down Woodward Ave. in her Mustang convertible into the motor city, with Bob Dylan playing on the radio. My straight blonde hair blew back in the wind. I wore bellbottom jeans that sat low on my hips with a huge brown leather belt that my brother-in-law had hand-tooled. My leather clogs had wooden soles. Those paychecks were great. I didn't have to ask Mom for anything.

For Christmas I had gotten a pair of silver wire sunglasses with large circular plastic inserts in five colors that could be interchanged. I was a product of the sixties and feeling good about myself. My heart belonged to my soldier, my high school sweetheart. I had my entire life planned out and it was going to be amazing.

Senior prom came and went, and I had no interest in going. Nobody asked me because they all knew I was taken. Besides, my junior prom had been a fiasco when I borrowed my cousin's dress and her dad, my uncle, had pitched a royal fit. The dress had been given to my cousin by her aunt who worked at *J. L. Hudson* and he said nobody was going to wear it but my cousin. My aunt and cousin convinced him to allow me to not only wear the dress but also her white bunny fur cape. So, for senior prom I knew I could not afford a dress and my parents never brought it up. I was fine not going.

Besides, I was busy thinking about my wedding. We would be married the week after my high school graduation at his Episcopal Church. Even my dad's family said they would attend. I found a beautiful ivory lace A-line dress at *Winkelman's*. Mom bought it for me. We also found an ivory pair of pumps a short veil and short gloves. I was so happy. It would be a perfect wedding picture standing alongside my husband in his army dress uniform. This marriage would work out perfectly and remove me from a difficult life,.

God had taken a very back seat in my life. I had taken control of my destiny by making decisions based on what felt good. Who else was going to help me? Nobody had stepped up. It was the mantra of the sixties. *"If it feels good, do it"*. I did make sure I was married in a church. I would follow my husband's religious beliefs like the dutiful wife, just as Mom had. He didn't attend church regularly, so neither did we as a couple.

In midst of the planning, I decided an office job seemed glamorous. I was tired of working weekends and nights at the grocery store. There was an ad for a placement service from *Snelling and Snelling Employment Agency* that captured my attention while searching the want ads. This was a Monday through Friday job, 8 AM to 5 PM. I decided to apply.

It was June 1967, a busy month with high school graduation, a wedding, and a possible new job all in one month. Although the ad called for a minimum age of eighteen, and I was five months shy, I applied and lied about my age.

When I arrived for the interview, there were five or six girls waiting ahead of me. I took a seat in the line of chairs where they sat by the large front window. Wow, I hadn't considered competition. Each girl was asked to come to a booth where they were given an application to complete by a male assistant manager. The second man would go over the application with the girl, and then finally the manager would enter the booth and ask the important questions.

Two girls didn't make it to the second interview. They gathered their things and left the office quickly. Not only did I make it to the manager, I was asked to demonstrate my typing skills. Sixty words per minute was the standard required in the ad. I had never typed a word in my life, not one.

I stared at the typewriter and thought to myself, this can't be that difficult. I knew how to operate a ten-key adding machine from balancing my drawer at the food store. How hard could this be?

When the manger discovered my lack of skill he came to the desk and said, "Here is a ream of paper. This is what I want you to do. Type your name and today's date at the top of the page. Type this paragraph with no mistakes. I don't care how long it takes."

I left four hours later in tears having completed the assignment.

The next afternoon I was offered a position as cashier at the loan company. The manager recognized something in me. This was a life-changing moment. After one year and testing me in different jobs, he asked me to consider the company's management-training course.

I accepted the challenge and embarked on a career that would last for twenty-eight years and take me around the world.

Someone, a man at that, was finally going to mentor me.

10

Married Life

THE WEDDING WAS HELD ON a Friday afternoon because my soldier only had a three-day furlough. We had invited my grandparents and uncles and aunts and of course his small family, all of them local. The ceremony was held at the Episcopal Church in town that his family belonged to. Everyone arrived on time for the 3 PM wedding.

He wore his army dress uniform, and I wore the A-line lace cage dress. My hair was a simple flip topped off with a "fall" of huge curls pinned into a crown sort of thing on top. We were a handsome couple, but I am sure the guests questioned how my parents could allow a marriage to such a young couple.

Mom and Dad threw a backyard barbecue for family and work friends to celebrate our nuptials. We left the party as soon as we could. We planned to honeymoon in Gatlinburg, TN, and needed to leave at the crack of dawn the next morning. We only had three days and we wanted to make the best of it.

Hubby was assigned to a military base just ten miles from where we lived. It was an underground army Nike missile base with high security. We rented a small upstairs flat in town for $200 a month. It was fun to use our wedding gifts. I felt like we were playing house, but this time, it was for real. I thought it was the happiest I had ever been. I had finally escaped the turmoil and felt completely in control of my life for the very first time. And, most importantly, I believed I had a man who loved me.

Sadly, it didn't matter the face of the groom. The face could have been anyone. And even more sadly, I had been led to believe I needed a man to escape from my horrible life. Did I love him? How does a seventeen-year-old know about love? I was in love with the idea of love, of marriage, and a life beyond my crazy family life.

I was creating my own Norman Rockwell life. It was no more real than the one I had lived so far.

The furnished apartment we had rented from a sweet little lady in her late seventies was clean and neat. She lived on the ground floor. It had dark wood floors and sparkling white walls. The small living room held only a sofa, two chairs, and three small tables. Across from the sofa was a white brick fireplace flanked by two high small wooden windows that could be opened to let in the fresh summer morning air. Located just a few blocks from my high school, I felt safe and independent when my groom had to stay on the army base nights.

Sunday, July 23rd, I awoke and made a pot of coffee and turned on the portable television with foil rabbit ears. National news reported trouble brewing downtown Detroit. Racial unrest was building, stemming from arrests made by Detroit City police in the early hours at a "blind pig" on the west side of the city.

Groups of Black protesters formed in the streets in the 12th Street district, an area Whites would typically avoid. Bottles and rocks were thrown at lines of policeman as they shielded themselves to control the crowds. It was all happening just an hour's drive from our tiny apartment in the city of Pontiac.

This went on for two days. Then Governor George Romney ordered the Michigan Air National Guard, and President Lyndon B. Johnson sent both the 82nd and 101st Airborne Divisions into the city. This was serious. Martial law was declared within and beyond city limits extending as far north as Pontiac, where I lived.

I was stuck in the apartment and my husband at the base for five days. I could hear gunshots as snipers shot from the roof of the cleaners just two blocks away. The news flashed images of looters climbing through broken store-front windows carrying TVs and electronics on their shoulders. Parked cars that sat along the streets were on fire, sending billows of black clouds into the blue skies. Military jeeps patrolled the street outside my windows.

When the disturbance ended, 43 were dead, 1,189 injured and 7,200 arrests had been made. More than 2,000 buildings had been destroyed. When my husband finally came home, we went for a drive into the city to see for ourselves the depth of destruction. It looked like a war zone. Even streets we had traveled for years where historic buildings met urban sprawl took on a war-like appearance. It was eerily disturbing.

It was a time of change. People were standing up for their rights. No longer were they going to be quiet. It was the sixties and there was a definite movement afoot.

While he was stationed at the local army base, we met a young married couple. She was a hair stylist and worked in a shop downriver near her parents.

Both our husbands' orders sent them to Korea. Thankfully they were not headed to Vietnam. We promised to get together at least once a week to keep busy while they were away.

We immediately struck up a bond.

11

While He Was Away

I MOVED BACK HOME WITH MOM to save money; however, between work, visiting my new friend and her family, I was seldom there on weekends. My new job was great. I really liked the hours, my fellow employees, and the work.

Occasionally, Dad would bring home dresses in just my size. He explained they were dresses one of his secretaries no longer wanted. Later I would find they belonged to her!

Once Dad came home with a super cute dog. The dog was a black mixed breed, maybe cocker spaniel and schnauzer. He was adorable and seemed to love Dad. He had a funny name, "Schmo"; I'd never heard anyone else use that name before except Dad. He claimed one of the workers at this office was moving into an apartment that didn't allow animals. He told them he would take the dog. But that dog sure seemed to like dad. On command, he would sit up, hold his paws together as if he was saying his prayers for a treat. He was fluffy and sweet.

My job at the loan company opened many doors for me. I opened a credit card at Winkelman's and purchased several outfits on credit. Oh, and of course a new winter coat.

The manager at my office continued to push me to learn new jobs. Soon I had progressed to bookkeeper. It was a great thrill when I could balance the ledger that included the old and new balances, the interest charged and principal. My new job was to type the figures from each column on the account cards and total them on the ten-key. I would hold my breath as I calculated the totals until they came out perfectly.

We were located just a few miles from the General Motors auto plant. Every Friday was payday, and the workers would line up after 3:30 with their paychecks making their payment and receiving the change, eager to drop by the bar on the way home for a cold one to start off the weekend. I was moving up and was excited to be on the manager training program for this large national finance company.

One day our AVP came to explain about a new computer system that could complete my bookkeeping report in less than five minutes. The cashiers input the payment amounts and the computer did the rest. The computer took their input and made a report even more in depth than I had done manually. I was asked to be on the team that would travel from office to office to train staff on the transition to this amazing computer system. It was encouraging to be selected to help with this innovative parallel project. Along with the request came a promotion.

I had tasted success, and I loved it. This manager training program was working out great.

12

California Here I Come

SIXTEEN MONTHS LATER, THE FELLAS returned from Korea. My friend and I were excited to get to the airport to greet them. His next tour of duty was San Francisco. I financed a shiny black SS 396 Chevelle as a coming-home present. Our plan was to pack up the car with his reel-to-reel Akai tape player, his Suzuki trail bike, our clothes, and my tambourine and off to California we would go far from the drama of life with Mom and Dad. We would caravan west with our friends to begin our life together.

There was a job waiting for me when we arrived in San Francisco. We would get pregnant right away and begin our family. I had it all worked out in my mind.

At nineteen, God was still far off in the distance of my rearview mirror. Truthfully, I just couldn't trust my life to something or someone I couldn't see. Faith sounded good, but was it real? I didn't truly understand God's love for me. I loved the safe and secure feeling attending mass gave me, but my husband was not Catholic, and I needed to submit to him just as I had been taught. I would figure all of this out later when things were more settled.

We found an apartment in Corte Madera close to the army base and used the bus transportation into the city. It was difficult to park the car in the expensive garages close to my office and I liked riding the bus across the Golden Gate Bridge and the short cable car ride to the office.

Just one month into our new adventure, to my delight, I was pregnant. My dreams were unfolding. I was excited to be expecting even though I was so far from family. After all, this was my family now.

He was stationed at Fort Baker, an army base situated just beneath the Golden Gate Bridge in Marin County. At twenty-one, I noticed a big change in my husband since he had been away. He worked three days on and two days off. He would party with his buddies, playing his tape player, smoking pot, and drinking.

Our small second-floor apartment walls were decorated with black-light posters. Plastic blowup furniture filled the living room overlooking the pool. When I would return from the city at night, he would be passed out on the floor or completely incoherent. I wrote it off to being in this messed-up military. I was certain he would step up once the baby arrived.

Viet Nam casualties were flown to Letterman General, a military hospital in the Presidio of San Francisco. It was June of 1969, and the conflict was raging. Draft dodgers protested in the streets as I walked to my office. I had such mixed feelings. I was proud of my husband for defending our country. But the politics of the conflict didn't make sense. The homeless along my route to the office were mostly drugged-up Vets missing legs and sleeping on the sidewalks. It was hard to see them forgotten by not only the government but also the people they had fought to protect.

You could hear the soft cling of finger cymbals and chanting of Hare Krishna followers just below my third-floor office window at the corner of Market and Powell. They would gather early in the day dressed in white robes, their heads shaved, panhandling for money when the SF Policemen were out of earshot. They were strange compared to the longhaired hippies that hung in Haight Ashbury just blocks away.

People's views were changing dramatically. Issues of war, feminism, civil rights, environmentalism, gay rights, and conservatism showed up in lyrics to songs. This was a far cry from the way our generation had been brought up not to discuss politics or religion outside of your home. It was acceptable to voice your opinion, and everyone did so proudly and loudly and sometimes with signs in protest groups. The government was overstepping its bounds and its young people were rebelling.

While my pregnancy was smooth, my marriage was not. The parties in our small apartment were more frequent; I always refused to participate and would close my bedroom door and lay on the bed. This baby was far too important to me. I didn't like what was going on, but I really didn't have a choice.

One day I returned home from work to several of his friends and music blasting. I confronted him, and an argument ensued. He punched me in the stomach, and I fell back on the bed. At that moment I knew he was not the kind, sweet boy I had fallen for. He was a drugged-up drunk. He and his friends would laugh and talk about the parties they had in Korea, about the women and the sex, and it was all just disgusting to me. I wanted to run, but I had nowhere to go. Of course, I didn't want to admit to my family that I might have made a huge mistake.

I threw myself into my job and counted the days until I would deliver our baby. There was an offer for early-out from the army if he would sign up for college. I longed to get back home to be near my sister as soon as possible after the baby arrived. He signed up for the program willingly because it meant he could get out of the army six months early. He really didn't want to go to school. The truth was he wanted to get back home to party with his old friends.

13

1970—Beautiful Baby Boy

MOM FLEW OUT TO SAN Francisco a few days before my due date. I was happy to see her, and we combed the city tourist spots, walking tirelessly to help bring on labor and the baby. I was on maternity leave, my due date was May 5th, just four days away. Saturday night, Mom and I went to the movies to see *True Grit* with John Wayne. As we sat in the theatre, I told her I felt a funny feeling.

That Sunday night we went to Letterman General, the military hospital in the city. The nurses confirmed the baby was on its way. I was admitted and excited to meet my new little angel. After several hours of not moving forward, they hooked me up to a Pitocin drip to speed things up. It was comforting to have Mom at my side.

My husband was on duty, so I left word for him to come. The labor was slow to progress. They hooked the baby to a monitor to check fetal distress. I had labored throughout the night, and I was beginning to get very tired. I seemed to be going in and out of consciousness and had no sense of time. The doctors continued to check me, but I wasn't progressing to their satisfaction.

Finally, the doctors were going to scan me to see if I had a pelvic obstruction. It was now Tuesday, and I was beyond exhaustion. They wheeled me down to radiology and placed me on a bed with a huge circular frame. As the frame started to roll, I was strapped to the bed but upright. The pressure and the unfamiliar position were unbearable. I thought I might be dying.

After the test was completed, they rolled me back to my room and suddenly there were nurses and doctors surrounding me, and Mom was asked to leave the room. My little seven-pound son was born. When they handed him to me, I wept tears of joy. Except for a huge red spot on his head from the monitor, he was perfect. His lungs were strong, and we both had made it through the difficult three-day labor. His father was passed out in the waiting room on a bank of chairs with a newspaper covering him like a homeless person as I bonded with my little angel son.

They kept me a little longer to make sure we were both recovered from the hard labor, but we were home for the weekend. We were going home. As I dressed him in his "going home" outfit, I remarked to Mom, "Is he really this cute or is it just because he is mine, I think he is so beautiful?"

She might not have been the most unbiased person to ask, but Mom nodded and smiled in agreement.

Sunday was Mother's Day and Mom, baby-daddy, and baby and I drove up into Muir Woods for a special brunch at a German deli with spectacular views. After lunch, we drove to Stinson Beach and sat on a blanket on the sand. Mom and my husband stacked the empty Coors cans as they enjoyed the windy spring day on the beach. When they topped the stack with an empty formula can, I told them it was time to get back.

The baby was adorable. He had managed to fight for three days to make it into this world, so I knew he was strong. I felt I had never loved anyone so much in my entire life. I was so happy and certain everything would work out.

We had six weeks until my hubby would be discharged. I had quit my job to be a stay-at-home Mom. We would get back to Michigan and we would make our plan. Baby-daddy had to go to college to fulfill his military commitment. We would figure it all out once we were back in Michigan.

Something deep within me reminded me it was important to have the baby baptized. I made the arrangements at the non-denominational church on base. Our friends from Michigan were asked to stand in as godparents. It was a simple but important service. I was going to protect this little guy and give him a perfect life.

14

Home Again

WE DROVE STRAIGHT THROUGH TO St. Louis from San Francisco at a marathon pace. A car bed in the back seat was perfect for the baby. We trailed a small U-Haul behind with our belongings. We were on our way home, and I was excited for everyone to meet our little son. We completed the trip and were home in just three days.

We bought a small new mobile home on a lot in a park just north of town. It was completely furnished and had a bright kitchen with shiny new appliances. I was proud of our new little home. I planted flowers and two green bushes in front.

Since I had gone on maternity leave from my job in San Francisco, I could take time figuring out what to do about work. In my dream plan, I would stay home and raise my son and probably future children. My dream wasn't exactly the reality we were living. I could always go back to work if I had to, but I was enjoying this time with my adorable son. He was perfect, and he was the most amazing thing that had happened in my life.

I made friends with the neighbors. There were about four Michigan State Police families living on my street. Mobile home living was perfect for them as they moved from duty stations across the state, moving their home right along with them. The husbands worked odd shifts, their wives and children were often home alone. They all had one or two children and we would have play dates. I considered their group to be family. They accepted Scott and me quickly.

My husband had taken a job at a factory owned by my brother-in-law. They were happy to help a returning Vet and work with his school schedule. Everything should have worked out great.

However, he wasn't attending classes or going to work. One day my sister made a most difficult call to say he hadn't come to work for two weeks and there wouldn't be a paycheck. How could this be? He would leave each morning with the lunch I had packed. He did stay out for beers with the guys, but I didn't think much about that. Where was he spending his days?

Those same feelings I had when I lived at home began to surface. The deceit, the lies, and the reality that he didn't want to be with his son and me was more than I could handle. I thought moving away from home and starting my own life was going to take that pain away.

One day a police officer came to the door. Our car had been involved in a hit and run accident and the mother who was driving the car with her two young children had taken down our license plate. "Where is the car?" he asked.

The next day I called around to find help with addiction. I made an appointment with a doctor. We both went to the appointment. He sat answering the questions and a physical examination was completed. After the examination the doctor called us back into her office. There was a medication that could be taken that would make him violently ill if he drank or took drugs. This was his only option. He refused. The doctor told us if he didn't want help, there was no way to force him to accept it. We left the office in silence.

I had tried everything I knew of to help him with his problems. He just wasn't willing to do his part. I had a child to consider. I had to make a move.

It was fall, my favorite time of year in Michigan. The leaves were turning, and the air was crisp. The Franklin Cider Mill had just opened for the season. My sister and I took Scott as a special treat. We bought a bag of donuts and a jug of cider and found a spot to picnic near the back of the mill. The smell of the apples and the fried donuts was amazing as we sat on the grass, orange leaves drifted in the clean fall breeze. I shared with her my deepest concerns. She was so strong and so kind to not judge me. She just listened until I was finished and was the total voice of reason.

I didn't have money for a divorce, but she was sure Grandma Amy would give me the $200 I needed for the attorney. The next day I visited Dad's mother and told her about my failure. She gave me the money without hesitation, and I made an appointment to see the divorce attorney.

15

Just the Two of Us

THAT WEEK, MY BEAUTIFUL SIX-MONTH-OLD son and I moved back in with Mom and Dad. Mom was happy to have a baby in the house again. Winter had set in, and on Sundays we would sit in the family room with the gas logs burning, the baby playing with his toys, and a beef roast in a pot on the stove. Dad sat in his easy chair puffing on his pipe as the aroma of Cherry-Blend tobacco encircled him. Here I was again back at home, a failure, but my parents had come through for me. At least my son and I had a roof over our heads.

My former boss welcomed me with open arms. I settled into a familiar routine, but this time, I had a child at home. My sister watched Scotty during the day. It was all working out.

During the past couple of months, I had dropped some weight and was not feeling so great. I wrote it off as being emotionally depleted from all that was going on. I visited my doctor. I was five months' pregnant.

This came as a complete shock to me. I had gotten very thin and missing a period here and there was not uncommon for me. But had it been five months?

Dad could see how facing my failures had affected me. He loved having his newest grandson in the house and encouraged me with my career at the finance office. He tried to be as supportive as possible when he was around.

When I told my parents I was pregnant, Dad said, "Look, the greatest joy you have had in your life so far has been your son. You are going to have another little joy. We will help you get through this."

His reaction touched me deeply.

But, a few days later, something was wrong. I was taken to the hospital and examined. I was losing the baby. The baby was just not strong enough. Something had gone wrong while it was forming.

At five months along, I had to go through labor and delivery. I lay in the hospital room alone while the pains continued for a few hours. It was all so confusing. Finally, the baby delivered right in the hospital bed. I remember looking down and seeing him on the sheet between my legs. He was perfectly formed, but blue and lifeless, another little boy. I was overcome by sadness. What had I done to deserve all of this? My life was in shambles. I could not even take care of my one son. Another would have been even more difficult. I prayed to God to help me with my life. I said the prayers I had been taught over and over as I lay in that hospital bed crying.

This was hitting the bottom of the trash heap for me. It is amazing what it takes for us to turn to God. We are so sure we can manage our lives without His divine help. But, when it seems there is no other way to turn, if we are fortunate to know about Him at all … we know we can turn to Him for help.

In the morning a dozen long-stemmed red roses arrived with a card from my dad. He said it would be all right. I fell asleep, and when

I awoke, I dressed and went home to be with my parents, back to my sweet son.

I dove into my career. My goal was to complete management training as quickly as possible. It was all up to me now with God's help.

Soon I realized my ex was not going to meet his child support obligations. He could barely take care of himself, let alone a family. This made it harder on me, but I was not surprised. I understood what alcohol addiction was and I was seeing first-hand how it controlled a person and forced them to make poor choices. Nobody needed to take care of us, I would provide for us all on my own.

In the spring, I was promoted to lending supervisor. It was great to be able to run the lending department of a small loan office. I was learning quickly and made recommendations for each loan and submitted them for the final approval of the manager. The manager was impressed when I upsold the loans with profitable credit insurance. A sense of accomplishment began to lift me from the dark hole I had been climbing out of for months.

Next, I was made collection supervisor. This was a more difficult area because it involved outside collections. Pontiac was an industrial town with plenty of public housing and some of the areas were unsafe. I had to prove, regardless of my gender, I could do the job as good if not better than my male counterparts. There was no stopping me. I had tasted success and I loved it. Well, truth was, I had something to be proud of ... I was a single mom and a rising career woman.

16

"Mr. MSP"

1971

O NE DAY TWO MICHIGAN STATE Police (MSP) officers came to the office. I was summoned by a cashier to come to the front. One of the men I had seen visiting my MSP neighbors. He lived behind me in the mobile home park. He had heard about my break up and wondered how I was doing. Completely caught off guard, I was nervous and didn't know what to say. He asked if I would like to go to dinner one night. Before I knew what was happening, I had accepted.

My mind was reeling. Questions were flying in my head. Was I ready for this? Things seemed to be happening very quickly. He certainly would not be a drug user. He had an upstanding job. What could it hurt?

Mr. MSP and I continued our relationship for five years before he asked me to be his wife. His family was wonderful and kind to my son and me. They were Catholic and lived in the upper peninsula of Michigan. His father was superintendent of schools. His mother was head of the school state lunch program. We visited them often and I loved them and his three sisters, all so accepting of me and my young child. They were such fun to be around and the kind of family I had always dreamed of.

I accepted his proposal and felt I had finally found a lasting love. We were married on the Black Rocks near Marquette. As I look back on this, I find it rather comical being married on the Black Rocks.

He introduced me to the sport of sailing. We bought a small *Hobie-Cat* to grasp the skills required to trim the sails and hike the waves across the beautiful freshwater lakes that surrounded us. Like most avid boaters, we soon stepped up to a larger boat, a twenty-two-foot sailboat had a cabin and a galley that allowed us a safe place for Scott to nap and where I could prepare food.

It was beautiful to be out on Lake St. Clair at dusk. I would often sit on the bow and watch the sun set in the gray and orange sky and if we were lucky enough to catch it, marvel at the phenomenon created by the action of the waves against the boat as it glided silently through the water. It is called phosphorescence. The bioluminescence of organisms in the surface layers of the wave create a magical starlike vision and added to the wonder and peace that drew me to life on the boat.

Soon, I was joining an all-female crew on a thirty-four-footer. We would compete in the SORC weekend qualifiers against all-male crews. We came in first place a lot of the time and our captain was known to be merciless. When we were forced to head off at the turn of the marker, she would never back down. It was a great feeling to be a part of this crew and it taught me a lot about being a member of a team.

One of Mr. MSP's sisters and her husband, both teachers, moved to St. Petersburg. The entire family would visit them frequently and enjoyed the long, lazy days on the white sandy beaches and two-hour dinners at great seafood restaurants. We loved the casual Florida life and would dream about moving there and taking our boat sailing in the beautiful Gulf of Mexico.

The regional manager for my company was making a visit to our office and when it was my turn to have a closed-door discussion with him, I entered the office and sat in the chair in eager anticipation of what he had to say. He was always a positive force and was a great representation of management within our Fortune 500 company. I admired everything about him. What he said next took me by complete surprise. He offered me the position of branch manager of the office. He explained changes were being made, and my current manager was needed in a larger office. He was confident I would be the perfect replacement. Along with the promotion came a sizeable increase as well as bonus incentives. I floated out of the office still uncertain this was not a dream. It was great to know this was something I had accomplished on my own.

There was a rustic Catholic Church not far from our home that we attended each Sunday. I wanted to rush to the church to give my thanks to God for providing this promotion. It was still too soon to enroll Scott in religious education classes, but I wanted my son to feel comfortable in church and to make it an important part of his life. The three of us attended mass each Sunday together. I felt a familiar peace come over me whenever we entered the church.

We spent off time partying with the other MSP families. There was always a lot of drinking and I found myself joining in. This didn't seem unusual to me. But there were many nights I would put the baby down and pass out on the bed, waking up groggy in the morning but never missing a day of work. My husband would continue to party on through the night with who knows who or what time he would come to bed.

He was extremely jealous of any male who showed me the least amount of attention. In my naivety I thought his green eye was a sign of deep love for me, that he wanted me for his own. But I would later realize this was just another sign of his unfaithfulness. He was the one who was insecure and needed to control every aspect of our relationship. He was flirting with and acting out with other women. He didn't like seeing his actions toward other women in the behavior of any man toward me.

Suspicion started to enter my mind about his faithfulness. I wrote it off as paranoia and went about our busy lives.

The job, while challenging, was very rewarding. I loved every minute of the competition between the other managers in the group. I won every contest, and bonus checks were a real plus.

Upon our return after a week of spring vacation in Florida, I wrote a letter requesting transfer with my company to St. Petersburg. My boss read the letter and said he would forward it to the regional director for consideration. But nothing ever became of it. I was thankful for my position and loved my job right where I was.

During the next two years, my husband worked as an undercover officer in the drug enforcement department of the MSP. He drove a soup-ed up Dodge, grew his hair long, and sported a goatee and mustache. His days were long. He left his wedding ring in the box on the dresser. He said he didn't want to risk his drug dealers learning he had a family.

He would often spend the day sailing on Lake St. Clair with his other undercover buddies. His boat was his office he said. It was all part of the plan. They would make drug deals and then place the guys under surveillance, reporting everything back to the detectives who would form a case to present to the prosecutor. It took months and numerous transactions to build the case against these suspected criminals. That was his job and he loved playing the edgy role of a drug dealer.

Weekends we would load up the car and drive out to the boat. We would take our son and provisions to the boat for the weekend. It was great spending sunny summer days drifting along the choppy blue waters of the lake, sunning, fishing, drinking, and playing music. Scotty, now three years old loved napping in the bow of the boat inside his comfy sleeping bag. Life was great again.

One early Saturday we stopped at the bait shop just a mile from the boat to pick up fishing supplies. We all three entered the shop and suddenly he motioned for me to take the baby and go directly to the car and get down on the floor of the car. I could tell by his demeanor he had encountered one of the dealers. So, I did exactly as I was told. He purchased bait while having a quick conversation with the clerk and the thug, returned to the car, and we sped off. This was the life he had chosen, and this was now our life too.

Often when we would go out for dinner, as I would excuse myself and visit the ladies' room, his 357-Magnum was tucked into my purse. I would see the gun in the mirror as I refreshed my lipstick. You can only imagine the look from the faces of ladies crowding the vanity.

I was proud of his profession, happy in my job, and so thankful to have a father for my son. We had a good thing going. And maybe just maybe we would make a move to sunny Florida.

17

Life With "Mr. MSP"

T HIS WAS THE MID-SEVENTIES AND Jimmy Hoffa had mysteriously disappeared, leaving his car in the parking lot of a fashionable suburban Detroit restaurant "Machus Red Fox," where, coincidentally, Dad often entertained clients.

The MSP worked closely with the FBI to solve the suspected homicide of this famous American labor union leader and former International President of the Teamsters Union with strong ties to organized crime.

Being an undercover DEA agent, my husband was privy to the Hoffa information in the event he heard anything relevant from his underworld contacts. He would study the mob organizational charts with pictures and real and fictitious names until he knew each one by heart.

While it was frightening to consider, it was also intriguing until the first day of kindergarten for my son.

Up early and ready with his lunchbox and school supplies, we headed out the front door to take a picture. As I turned to close and lock the door behind me, I shuddered. Written on the door in red lipstick were the words *We will get you*. That was the first of many days we were escorted to and from work and school by an MSP patrol car.

Uncertain where the message had originated, all precautions were taken. While my son enjoyed sitting on his lunch box in the front seat of a patrol car, I was less than pleased to be required to call a patrol car to escort me on my daily bank deposit runs and anywhere else my job might take me. It was beginning to frighten me.

Then one day shortly after this, there was trouble at the MSP post. A woman met with the post lieutenant accusing my husband of fathering her child. They asked for his badge so that no disgrace would befall the department. He turned it in and came home to explain. Suddenly, my world began to crumble once again.

I wanted to run, to get as far away from him and from my family and friends as possible. How could I have failed once again? I was so ashamed that my second marriage was now falling apart. And I was broken-hearted.

That day I decided to fly to Florida to find a job. I arranged for my mother to care for the baby. My sister-in-law and her husband offered for me to stay with them until I was settled in a job and able to sort everything out. I could send for my son. They would help us make a new home in a new place far away from all the madness.

While explaining to my boss that I needed a week of vacation to look for a job in Florida because nothing had ever become of my transfer request, wheels started moving. Within an hour I received a call from the Florida Regional Vice President asking where in the state I wanted relocation.

When I explained I had family in St. Petersburg he said, "What great luck, I have need of a manager in Clearwater, just half an hour away."

Great, I had a job and a place to stay. I began to lay my plans to move, to leave my husband, and take my son to begin a new life as a single mom once again, frightened, but confident in my decision.

JKB (Mr. MSP) was hitting rock bottom. What I had suspected all along was true. His penchant for other women had destroyed his career and now his marriage. I didn't worry about him. I had gone into survival mode, something I was all too familiar with. I had a son to worry about. He could figure his own problems out. His family would be devastated.

I packed a large suitcase with work clothes and a few casual items, and toiletries. The large suitcase easily bungee corded to the rack on the trunk of my MGB. Kissing my little angel an interim goodbye, I drove south with the top down and determination in my mind. At least my boy would be in good hands while I started my new job and looked for a home for us to stay.

As I drove south on I-75, tears flowed down my cheeks until I reached the Florida border.

18

Sunny Florida Life

THERE WAS TIME TO GRIEVE once I crossed the Michigan border. I wondered what was so wrong with me that I was not good enough, why I couldn't be the object of a man's desire and love. It was a dark trip south on I-75 until I reached the causeway connecting Tampa with Clearwater about twelve hours later.

The sun was shining brightly as I crossed the narrow strip of land lined with palm trees. Tanned families leaned against parked cars as they watched their children play in the shallow blue-green water of Tampa Bay. The sky was the bluest I had ever seen, the water just as I had remembered it, and the sand as white as sugar. I felt a sense of calm and renewed strength as I breathed in the salt air. It was going to be okay. I would see to it my son and I would be okay. I could make it on my own. I was just sure of it.

The Regional VP greeted me when I arrived and installed me officially as the branch manager of the office. I received a warm reception from the staff and soon I sat alone in my office. I was a bit apprehensive but excited to begin yet another new chapter in my life and thankful for family who loved my son that could help me figure out his childcare.

Constant phone calls interrupted my day from my ex-husband. He was asking to join me and if we could start anew. He would make it all up to me.

He was sorry.

I tried to be strong and not fall for his bag of deceitful promises. But his draw was strong. He had adopted my son and he wanted to be the family we had dreamed. I wanted to be a family. I wanted the life I hadn't lived for both Scotty and me. I didn't want to be the twice divorcee, with a son. How could I find a good man willing to take on such heavy baggage?

So, I took the path of least resistance. I allowed him back into our lives once more. He drove down with his belongings and arranged for his sailboat to be trailered down as well.

After a few months, we purchased a single-story condo on Tampa Bay in Clearwater just fifteen minutes from my office. He had taken a job with US Home as a building superintendent based on his experience during college. He was trying to make a new life for our little family. We were slowly moving in the right direction.

We joined the local parish and enrolled our son in CCD classes. Scott received his First Holy Communion in the spring. We brunched at his favorite restaurant, 94th Arrow Squadron to celebrate. I was so happy he could receive the sacraments I had never been able to participate in. He was a real Catholic and I felt good knowing I was bringing him up to know God and be a part of a church family.

I prayed that God would heal our marriage. Time would tell if He heard me.

My job was moving along great. The office was producing great results receiving recognition from upper management. Competition at the group and regional levels pushed us to reach numbers never met. The staff got into it, and I did my best to recognize their successes with drinks after work. I felt the move had been a positive step in my career. Now if my marriage would survive, that would be the true test.

My son was having difficulty in school, and it was recommended he be tested. The test proved he had a learning disability, dyslexia. This is a shock for any parent to hear. But the school system would be able to help us. He didn't see the words the way we saw them. This required him to go to special classes where they would teach him to learn in a different way than the other children. He seemed to handle this without any problem. He was always an easy child, not acting out like others with his learning problems might have done. He handled the transition without hesitation. I wanted him to have whatever he needed, and the school system provided Title IV, back then giving every student whatever was required in all aspects from transportation to curriculum and special attention.

One day I received a phone call from my husband telling me I would be having some people stop by the office on their way from the Tampa Airport. One of the MSP Detectives we knew well called to ask a favor. He was flying a woman and her two children down from Detroit. The lady had been placed in the witness protection program and needed someone to watch out for her. My husband had earlier arranged for her to stay in a condo in our development paid for by the state of Michigan. He told me I should keep them in my office until he could get off work to escort them to the rented condo.

When they arrived at my office it was like a scene from a movie. The detective was dressed in a gray suit, white shirt, and tie. He accompanied a gorgeous blonde with a boy and girl about eight and nine, just a few years older than my son. The mother was dressed in a winter coat and fur hat. Someone had not told her that her secret hideaway was in a tropical climate. They stuck out like tourists and the office staff was left wondering what was going on as I escorted them to my office and closed the door.

They shared with me the details of her successful escape as if I were a trusted employee. I listened as if I were playing a role in some detective movie. It was all just bizarre.

Soon my husband appeared, and they followed him to the apartment complex. And she was introduced to her new surroundings. He assured her he would take good care of them. She and her children could feel safe.

He was done with the MSP. Hadn't they let him go in disgrace? The detective was his friend and felt my husband would be a good person to watch out for this important witness who had a photographic mind and could recite verbatim conversations she had overheard at the restaurant, *The Old Mill Tavern*, where Hoffa and his friends often spent the evening. The restaurant where she was their waitress turned friend joining the group after her shift. It was a dangerous favor I could not believe anyone could ask of us.

Rules had to be established early on. I was not her new girlfriend. They would not be joining us for dinner and our children were not playing together. This was a temporary situation, and I could not wait for it to be over.

Fortunately, within a month she and her children were moved into a house several miles away. It was over and nothing had happened that I could see.

It was early May 1978 and Mom was visiting. We were up early to prepare for the day. I remember Mom standing at the ironing board.

Scotty was sitting at the table eating his breakfast as I dressed for the office. The windows were open, and a steady tropical breeze blew through the condo from Tampa Bay to the street. We chuckled as the shirt that mom was ironing for my husband was flying off the board as she pressed each sleeve. The sky was dark and an odd color of pink, but no sun peered through the clouds that were sailing quickly across the sky. The TV reported thunderstorms in the forecast, certainly nothing unusual for a Florida spring day.

I had to get to the office early as auditors were expected from the home office in Texas. I waved as Scotty stood just outside our door waiting for the school bus.

The auditors were there when I arrived waiting in their cars for me to unlock the office. I chatted with them and set them up at a desk and began bringing them the reports and the documentation they would review. They were not conversational at all, so I retreated to my office as the other employees arrived, all of them discussing the weather of the morning.

A phone call came in for me. I answered in a pleasant voice with my name and asked what I could do. It was *witness protection girl* from Michigan calling to tell me my son's school just across the street from her house had been hit by a tornado and a third of the building was gone.

In disbelief I immediately dialed the school office. Busy, busy, busy. The sky was now black, and I knew I had to go to the school to confirm my son was okay. Radio reports revealed many of the students had been taken to local hospitals. Panicked, I told the auditors I would be back in a bit and left the office, heading directly to the school.

The main road to the school was blocked by a police officer. I drove my small MGB along the sidewalk past the gridlock of traffic toward the officer in his yellow slicker. "My son is in the school, and I must find him," I pleaded.

"Drive to the community college building that backs up to school property. Most of the students have been taken there, unless he was taken to the hospital, and they will call you," he shouted.

Call me? I was not waiting for the hospital to call me. I drove to the community college building and ran inside dodging mud-puddles along the way.

Once inside the dark cafeteria, the students sat at tables accompanied by an adult. They were eating peanut-butter sandwiches and milk served by staff. A gentleman dressed in a clown suit stopped at a table and performed some magic tricks. Some of the children were wrapped in blankets. Some were weeping, and the room was quiet considering the number in the room. At the front of the cafeteria stood a police officer on top of a lunch table with a bullhorn and a clipboard. A long line of bewildered parents streamed along the wall waiting to hear the officer call the name of their child hoping they would answer. It was surreal.

There was no way I was going to stand in that line and wait to see if my son would answer the call. I strolled about the lunch tables in the dark looking for my angel. Along the way I saw some of his classmates and some of the neighbor children. Finally, there he was sitting at the end of the table. As I approached him, with an adult volunteer at the table looking me square in the eyes, he said, "Hi Mom" in the happiest tone I had ever heard. I got the message and tried hard to hold back my tears of relief as I hugged my little boy.

He told me to go to any of the officers and be sure to give them his name, so they knew where he was. As I did this, the officer asked me if I could recall any other children in the cafeteria. I gave him their names and whisked my son out and into the car.

I drove home and Mom told me to put Scotty in a warm bath to calm him. He appeared to be in shock. We did so and told him it was going to be all right.

The wing where his classroom was located had been completely leveled. Later he shared his experience of that day. He told us how the class had left the room and went to the lunchroom just a few minutes before it hit. He was told to get under the lunch table. Next to him was his classmate crying and screaming and he told her to shut up. He saw a tree fly by the window and heard loud noises everywhere. He was completely terrified.

We soon learned that two children had died and ninety-five hospitalized. One of the fatalities was that little classmate's brother. He was in kindergarten, and it was his birthday. His present, a new bike, was waiting for him in the garage at home. My son never got over this experience. To this day, he is frightened of storms and gathers his family together in one room when weather takes a turn for the worse.

The office called and the auditors wanted me to come back so they could close out with me. I explained what happened, but they needed to be on to the next office and they asked me to come in regardless. I did so and sat in my chair behind my desk as they explained the exceptions they had found, never attempting to supply the supporting documentation that would negate the violation. They left the office. And I returned home to calm my son.

The next morning, after the devastation of the tornado hit national television, I received a call from my regional VP apologizing for the auditors. They had no idea what had taken place in my life that day.

19

Atlanta

THE REGIONAL VP VISITED THE office each quarter to review the operation, audits conducted annually, and training directors visited when new programs were rolled out. Everyone was on a training program. As manager, it was my responsibility for every aspect of the office, cashiering, bookkeeping, collections, new business, insurance sales and claims follow-up, solicitation, training and HR hiring and firing. My personal reviews were always positive.

It wasn't long before I was promoted to the training department at the regional office in Atlanta, GA. Management assured me this job was a steppingstone, resulting in a promotion to AVP in charge of seven offices in West Florida including the office I had managed. Travel was required.

During dinner I explained to my husband what the promotion entailed. While it did require me to move to Atlanta it would be for just three months. I would work there during the week and drive back to Clearwater on Friday night. This was very important to me. Our son was in grade school and his aunts who now lived nearby could help with after school care. He saw the excitement and knew I had been working toward this for several years. It was a step to the group job that would bring us more money. He agreed we could work it out.

After arriving in Atlanta, I found a room for rent in a house near Stone Mountain. I explained I would be traveling and seldom if ever there on the weekend. I moved in and began my new job as training coordinator.

Just as management had promised, within three months I was back in the Clearwater office, but this time as the group AVP and I had a secretary. It was amazing to me that I had achieved this accomplishment. I was happy to be back home with my sweet son and his father.

Then the phone calls started. The phone would ring, and I would rush to answer. As soon as I would say hello, the person on the other end would hang up. It happened just about every night.

We bought a great house in a golf course community from his company at a discount and moved in just before the school year started. The mortgage payment was large because it was 1980 and rates were at an all-time high. But we would be able to handle it together.

We joined the local parish and started attending mass regularly. It was important for Scotty to continue CCD and receive his sacrament of confirmation.

My husband's company was having a lavish holiday party and I assumed we would be attending, so I searched for a sexy dress to wear. The night of the party he told me he was going alone. I was tired and confused, but not too disappointed. Scott and I spent the night with popcorn and TV.

The next morning, he arrived home. I had worried the entire night. He had no explanation and acted as if it was not important. My mind wandered and I was heartsick, but I carried on through Christmas as if nothing were wrong.

Could this be happening again? The phone calls were some sort of signal. I noticed he would disappear shortly after each one. I hated where my mind would take me. But, one day I confronted him, and it came spilling out. He was having an affair. I told him to be gone by the time I returned home from work. And he was.

The minute I returned home from the office I ran to the walk-in closet of our bedroom. The right side of the closet was filled with my clothes. The left side was empty. He was gone. I dropped to the floor and sobbed, faced with instant uncertainty. Once again, I was alone with my son and a failure.

This time there was no turning back. It was over.

But there was also an odd sense of peace within me. No longer would I have to live under a veil of suspicion or fear that I would say or do the wrong thing. I finally felt I was in control, and while everything around me appeared uncertain, it was relief I felt.

He purchased a sailboat large enough to live on and worthy of sailing long distances. He quit his job or perhaps was fired, I don't know the details, or did I really care. But shortly after the separation, he sailed off not telling anyone he was leaving. Of course, he had a female companion, a married woman who had left her husband and children to explore the Caribbean on his new floating home.

He had disappeared completely. Not a dime of child support was ever paid for the son he had adopted. But, also gone were the lies and the horrible emotional abuse we both suffered at his hands. We were far better off alone.

My son was devastated. This was the only father Scott had known. While he had been raised with an iron fist and a violent temper, he had never been physically abused. I was sure of that. Sometimes though, emotional abuse reaches deeper than a punch to the gut or a jab to the head. So, I made an appointment with a psychologist to help me explain to my son all that had happened. He felt like he was to blame for his father leaving, that he must have done something wrong.

Only two appointments were necessary. The first hour was with my son and I together, the second with me alone. My son seemed to listen and once I explained how we would not have to move or change our routine, he seemed to be okay with it. I, on the other hand, needed to know what was wrong with me? Why could I not keep a man? Why was I not good enough?

His answer, "You, my dear, are a poor picker." Those words resonated in my mind for many years. He was right. The one thing I could do to make a better choice was to pray about it, ask the Holy Spirit to give me direction.

It had been difficult for me to turn the entire control of my life over to someone I could not even see. I loved the idea, but was it truly possible? We were talking about more than me, it was my son who I loved more than myself here.

This was a turning point. I was done with men. I prepared a budget and realized if I didn't turn on the air conditioner or heat too high, controlled my food shopping, and didn't buy any clothes, I might be able to make it on my own salary. And thank God for my understanding sister-in-law who lived just around the corner who would care for Scott until I got home from the office and when I had to travel. She loved Scott and I could trust her to care for him. It would be tough, but we could make it.

Mom and I would speak over the phone weekly. I would call Dad at work, the only way I could catch him, maybe once a month. Things didn't seem to be going very smoothly for them.

My brother had signed up for a tour in the navy. My parents were happy about that as he had quit school and really started to act out drinking, chasing girls, and more they didn't want to talk about. He didn't have any direction in his life. They agreed the military would straighten him out after his naval basic training. He was stationed in Hawaii.

Mom and Dad had separated. They sold the family home and moved into an apartment. Soon after the move, they split up. I was not surprised by this news.

Mom was working with her sister as a hostess at a bar she owned downtown Detroit. My uncle had purchased the bar shortly before he died of a heart attack at the young age of thirty-eight. His wife, Mom's sister, felt she could run the bar and have some income to raise her two girls. It seemed like a logical solution to the two of them. But I knew the environment wouldn't be good for Mom, who was heavily drinking every day.

Thinking about my mother, I invited her to come stay with us. This seemed to be a good solution. The environment of my aunt's bar was not good in her mental state she was in. I could work and travel with my job, and Mom could watch over Scott and the house.

Mom and her sister drove her car down. They spent a couple of days together enjoying the area. But Aunt Lil had to return to her bar. It was fun having Mom with us at first. She met the neighbor next door and the two of them hit it off from the start. Her love of gardening prompted her to move around some of my bushes, not always where I wanted them, as she weeded and planted flowers to keep herself busy during the day. Mom kept the ironing bin empty, and Scott's room organized and clean.

Doesn't this sound wonderful? Well, the truth was the neighbor and Mom would begin the morning with fresh squeezed orange juice plus about half a glass filled with Vodka. By the time I got home, she was at the neighbor's pool bar continuing to party late into the night. Scott would check in with her periodically, but she wasn't in the house helping with his homework.

As I lay in bed, I could hear their voices as I tried to sleep. Sometimes Scott would creep into my bed saying he couldn't sleep. We would snuggle and I would reassure him everything was going to be okay.

When Mom started going to happy hour with the neighbors and coming home to the pool bar next door with gentlemen she had just met, I began to get uncomfortable. Now I had two humans to worry about. This was not working out. I called my aunt in Michigan and asked her to fly down with a ticket I had purchased and drive Mom back home in her car. Mom wasn't happy about my decision to "throw her out" but she had no choice. Finally, the house was silent again, a welcome silence.

My sister and her family were doing fine in Michigan. Her daughter, an overachiever with a perfect GPA, graduated from nursing school and began her medical career. We were so proud of her. Her son, on the other hand, seemed to be following the same path as my brother. But I chalked it up to being young men not able to find their direction yet.

After one year, I found it possible to balance Scott, my money, and my job with the help of my ex-sisters-in-law. My career continued to climb, and the bonus incentive checks allowed me to buy us both new clothes and even take a trip to the Cayman Islands. It was working.

Scott was still having difficulties in school and required tutoring after classes. I planned for the help he needed. My ex-sisters-in-law were teachers and one lived three houses down. She would tutor Scott after school and make sure he did his homework until I got home from work.

It was also recommended he find something that he could excel in other than schoolwork. He started out in band with a trumpet. That wasn't it.

Next, he joined the swim team at the community pool within walking distance from the house. He was a good athlete, enjoyed competition, and didn't complain about early swim practice. He won plenty of ribbons and it was fun for both of us to travel on Saturdays to local meets. It was a good life, and we were finally together after my long hours during the week.

We attended mass every Sunday and I thanked God for being able to stay in the house and for my son. I loved him so much and wanted to keep as much stability in his life as I could. I would do whatever it took to stay in the house, keep him in his familiar school and surrounded by the friends he had made.

20

The Stroke

I T WAS MARCH 16TH, DAD'S birthday, and I made my usual call to his office. The secretary Dad had for years answered.

"Hi, just me calling to wish my dad a happy birthday," I said.

There was silence on the other end.

Finally, she spoke, "Honey, didn't you know? Your Dad has been in William Beaumont Hospital for ten days. He suffered a stroke at his desk."

I was in shock and truly don't recall what happened next. But I called my sister who lived near Mom in Michigan, to ask her what was going on. She had just made the same birthday call. She or Mom had not been informed.

I phoned the hospital and they put me right through to his nurse. Dad was unable to speak. The massive stroke had left him paralyzed on the left side and he was in very poor shape. Years of fast living, smoking, eating, and drinking had finally caught up with him. The nurse asked if I would like to speak to his wife. Assuming she was speaking of my Mother I said, "Yes."

The moment she answered the phone I knew it was not my mother.

I had never spoken or seen Dad's mistress, but she was on the phone with me.

"Hello, Judi," she said in a scratchy, high-pitched voice as if she had known me my entire life.

I refused to speak to her and asked for the nurse, requesting she place the phone to Dad's ear, which she did.

"Dad, do you want me to come?" I asked through uncontrollable tears. He made a labored groaning sound.

The nurse said, "He does want you to come."

"Tell him I will catch the next plane," I replied.

After I planned for my son, I was on the next flight to Detroit. My sister was waiting as I walked out of the gateway at Detroit Metro. We drove directly to the hospital, as she brought me up-to-date on what was happening. She had called Mom to see if she knew the news. She did not. Of course, she was frantic. Regardless of what Dad had ever done, Mom loved him deeply. Mom was heading to the hospital right away.

When we reached Dad's room in the CCU, we could hear commotion. Mom was on one side of the bed, and "she" was on the other straining over his limp body yelling at one another. It was like a scene from a soap opera. The nurses on the floor were trying to neutralize the situation while Dad lay there with tubes and wires running from his body.

We pulled Mom from Dad, and my sister whisked her off to a rest room nearby while the "other woman" was escorted to the elevator. I was alone with Dad. Tears were running down his cheeks and it was clear he could not talk. I tried to calm him. Why hadn't someone called us? Why did we have to wait ten days to find out our dad had almost died? Who did this woman think she was and what kind of hold did she have on him?

A few minutes after Dad was stabilized, I entered his room calmly. I went to the bed and sat next to him reaching for his hand.

"Dad, you need to tell me somehow who you want to take care of you, Mom or her?"

His eyes seemed to search mine and he tried to speak but only an unrecognizable sound escaped.

I said, "Mom?" a strong question in my voice.

His eyes told me immediately "No."

I confirmed, "Squeeze my hand if you do not want Mom to take care of you."

He squeezed with his right hand.

I said "Okay, I will tell Mom and we will get her out of here."

The bathroom was down the hall, and I could not hear any sounds from outside. I opened the door and found Mom and my sister deep in conversation. I told them both, Dad had chosen the other woman to take care of him and not her. It was the most difficult thing I had ever said to her. Mom immediately turned violent, arms thrashing. We could barely control her.

"Let's get out of here."

We tried to calm her once more and told her we would talk this through somewhere else.

I spent three days with my sister and mother. We all were filled with spite for the woman. I was unsure of how I felt about Dad at that moment. I never went back to the hospital. Dad had made his choice and it clearly wasn't for us.

A few days later we heard our uncle, Dad's only brother had visited the hospital and at his suggestion arranged for an attorney to begin divorce proceedings. Their forty-year sham of a marriage was over, and the other woman had finally won.

21

Scott and Street Basketball

1983

FALL WAS APPROACHING AND POP Warner football signup was advertised on a small sign on our way out of the neighborhood. My sweet Scotty, now twelve, said he would like to join up. I jotted down the number and called when I had the chance. We would give football a try.

He got his equipment, and we laughed as he tried it all on. I took him to the sporting goods store to buy an athletic cup, belly-laughs. It was difficult not having a man to help with these things. But we did pretty well on our own.

I did go on an occasional date. My secretary pressed me to have dinner with her husband's partner in the CPA firm. She warned to be on the lookout for men who might be looking for someone to take advantage of. This was new. I never viewed myself as someone men might want to latch on to financially, a good catch. But I now had a house and a successful career and looked pretty good for thirty-two.

He was nice enough. I found him asking to go "Dutch treat." This CPA was really concerned about his bottom line, more important than being the gentleman I would have preferred.

Dating was difficult. Everyone seemed to have an agenda. By the time I figured it out, I had wasted precious time. I was over it and didn't have time for the games or the disappointment. The effort outweighed the slim possibility I could find someone who shared my views, desires, and character requirements.

Some nights the neighbors would invite me over to have a glass of wine or a beer and share a meal. That was pretty much my social life.

My work friends were almost family to me. We spent a lot of time together, and I truly cared about most of them. There was not a lot of opportunity to make friends anywhere else. Many of them had worked with me for years. And I was thankful for each of them.

My sad attempts at dating failed every time. I concluded it was easier to take it one day at a time not to worry about finding someone to share my life with romantically. I had my son. I could be perfectly content.

One evening several neighbors had gathered in a front yard across the street and as I pulled the car in the drive coming from work; they waved, summoning me to join them for a cold beer. I changed from my work clothes to something comfortable and walked over.

It was a Friday evening and Scott had a friend over. I told him to check in with me frequently. It was nice to relax with this group of neighbors. They decided to grill out, everyone brought a dish, and before long we had a great spread. The kids grabbed paper plates and went into the house to eat while the adults sat around the pool and shared stories.

This became a regular occurrence. Our tiny street had some interesting characters. It was fun to get to know them and made me feel a little safer living in that house with just my son. They all looked out for me. And it was something to do besides staying at home.

The Italian family across the street was especially nice. They had a daughter just a year older than Scott and a boy a few years younger. The husband was in sales and handsome with his thick black hair. He was extremely funny and had a great personality. The wife, a dental hygienist, was a great cook. They were very friendly and treated everyone as family.

"Mr. Soprano" told me his twenty-four-year-old nephew was moving down from Ohio to get a job in sales. He knew I had a lot of single teacher friends and asked me to take him out for drinks some night after work to introduce him. I agreed.

A few weeks passed and one evening as I was pulling into the driveway, I noticed an unfamiliar guy playing street basketball with my son. He was tall and shirtless, exposing his chiseled torso. He went for a layup but slowed thankfully, as he approached my twelve-year old son. They both came running as I turned off the car. He introduced himself and I thanked him for asking my son to play. It was a short encounter, but I was glad to meet him and noticed he had the same voice and charm as his uncle as well as a killer smile.

Engrossed in my work and busy life as a single mom, time passed. I hadn't thought to invite my new neighbor out as I had promised until one Saturday in late October. My former sister and brother-in-law were throwing a Halloween party at their house. This was the perfect opportunity to introduce "*Mr. Tall-Young and Handsome*" to my single teacher friends.

He was shooting baskets when I pulled my car out of the driveway on our way to my son's football practice.

"Listen, how would you like to come to a Halloween party with me tonight? Got any plans?" I asked.

"Sounds like fun," he immediately replied.

The details were shared.

"You are in charge of costumes. I'll be home around 5 PM."

"Ok," he replied as we sped off.

This was the perfect plan. I would be satisfying my neighbor's request of introducing him to my single girlfriends and if it didn't work out, he could easily leave without any fuss.

I went through the day running errands and spending precious time with my boy. Saturdays and Sundays were our time, and I treasured every minute.

When we finally reached the house, we both unloaded the groceries. I made us a bite to eat as I explained my plans for the evening. I was going to a party at Kathy and Dave's and would be close by. He could drop in as he wanted, but after dark, he must be home and settled in for the night.

He was a good boy. I think he had witnessed life with *Mr. State Trooper*, and he wouldn't think of causing me any further strife. His goal was to please me and help me and he did that most of the time. He was respectful and kind.

When Scott was tested at his teacher's suggestion by a child psychologist and diagnosed with a visual perception problem that caused dyslexia and placed in special classes since he was seven, I was devastated. His teachers all liked him and complimented him for being a leader in the class. He seemed to gravitate to the most difficult kid and encourage them to pay attention and do what was asked. His grades were good considering his limitations. He just needed to be instructed in a different way. It was great he could spend his afternoons with Kathy, his aunt who was a special education teacher helping him complete his homework. God must have been watching out for him with this perfect solution to a potential disaster.

Everyone who met Scott and got to know his sweet spirit, loved him. He was my greatest gift in life so far.

22

Trick or Treat

THE DOORBELL RANG. THERE HE stood, tight jeans and a black tee shirt with the words "SLAVE" in orange across his chest. He handed me a bag.

"Just put on this tee shirt with a pair of tight jeans."

The black tee-shirt read "MASTER" in orange lettering.

The innuendo was seductive as well as assuming. I gave him credit for creativity. I did as he requested, and we walked across the street to his temporary home to have a pre-party cocktail with his aunt and uncle.

They were always welcoming people. Kids, followed by a large spirited Irish Setter, ran through the house filled with the aroma of garlic. The Sunday sauce simmered on the stove in preparation for the next day's dinner.

We stood at the kitchen counter as his uncle pulled out a bottle of Ouzo from the liquor cabinet. He poured us each a shot glass full and made a toast to a good evening ahead.

"Salute," he said.

Never wanting to disappoint, I threw back the clear liquid. The warmth immediately permeated my throat.

"Oh … that was terrible," I shouted as everyone burst out laughing.

Shortly after we walked the short block to the party house. I felt completely relaxed and comfortable with my new friend. After all, that was all he was, someone I was going to introduce to a group of single teachers at a neighborhood costume party. This was certainly not a date.

When we arrived at the door, Kathy and Dave welcomed us with a hug as I introduced them to *Mr. Tall, Young, and Handsome*. She pointed toward the kitchen. We oohed and awed at the Halloween decorations. Kathy was a crafty one and always right on point with decorating. The kitchen was already filled with couples and groups of single girls in cute costumes. I introduced him to several guests as we both grabbed a drink. I took him on a tour of the house glasses in hand.

We ended up in a quiet part of the house away from the crowd, but not noticeably too far. We never spoke to anyone else all night. I don't clearly remember walking home, but I do recall checking my sons' bed to be sure he was asleep, that motherly instinct ingrained in me.

And I do remember him kissing me.

When I awoke in the morning, I tried to recall the events of the evening. Embarrassingly I couldn't. My head throbbed and I realized I had slept through mass. Scott came jumping onto the bed.

"Jeez Mom, get up, it's almost noon."

The doorbell rang and he ran to answer.

As he opened the door, I heard him say, "I can't play basketball right now, Tommy"

Tommy explained, to his surprise, that he had come to see me.

I rushed to the sink to brush my teeth. He burst into my bedroom.

"*Officer and a Gentleman* starts in an hour. What do you say we take in a matinee?"

He had a solution for every one of my excuses. And something in me said, "It's ok." I told him I would be ready in half an hour.

The entire time I showered and dressed I was in a fog about leaving the party and what happened after that. I felt embarrassed to be so out of control.

Many nights I would have a drink to dull the loneliness and guilt I harbored. What was wrong with me that I couldn't hold on to a man? Even my own Dad chose another woman over me. Now I had been through two husbands and they were gone one to drugs and one who couldn't keep his hands off other women. It was disturbing and humiliating. My self-esteem was pretty much non-existent. And how would all of this affect my young son? Did he blame himself for any of this? Now I was drinking to dull the pain, just like my mother! I was asking myself could I have a drinking problem? Just add that to the ocean of reasons why I was undesirable.

Truly, if it had not been for the success of my job, I don't know what my future would hold.

And now, I had a twenty-four-year-old unemployed guy asking me to the movies on a Sunday afternoon.

23

An Officer and a Gentleman

WHEN TOMMY ARRIVED AT MY doorstep, before the movie date, he looked amazingly handsome with that gorgeous smile and a confidence you couldn't help but notice. He escorted me to the car and off we went. Well, to my car, as he didn't own a car. In fact, he had nothing really.

At the local multiplex Tommy purchased two tickets to *"An Officer and a Gentleman."* He grabbed a drink, two straws, and a large bucket of popcorn at the concession stand and we made our way to the theatre already filled with moviegoers.

The movie had just recently been released and received great reviews. It was a "chick flick." So, the fact that Tommy even wanted to take me showed he was more than willing to please.

Put Richard Gere in a uniform and I am certain most women would bubble over with excitement. Debra Winger with her throaty voice and "girl next door" looks, perfectly cast for the factory worker on the search for a navy man who would offer her a ticket out of this small military town and perhaps even travels around the world.

There were some great scenes in the movie like the steamy hotel scene and the fight. The coup de grâce was the final scene as Zach Mayo, in his whites, marches toward Paula on the line, swoops her up, and carries her out of the factory never to return. Her fellow workmates cheered loud and long and even people in the small theatre joined in. As the credits rolled, we stood, and suddenly Tommy picked me up in complete *Mayo* fashion and carried me toward the exit. The cheers in the theatre were even louder, and for us!

Cheesy as it was, this was one of the reasons I later allowed myself to fall in love with him.

The next stop was a small table at *Bennigans'* where we shared our life's stories over a couple of beers and margaritas, and chicken nachos. He had a great sense of humor and I adored that. It had been a long time since I had laughed this hard. He told me his life desires were few and simple. He wanted to find a wife and form a large family. In practicality he admitted he could be happy anywhere even in a cardboard box under a bridge with the right person. He was searching for the love of his life to marry and raise a huge Italian family living happily ever after.

Just before we left the table he said, "Someday, I am going to marry you."

Was he asking me to consider enlisting in his dream as *Mrs. Tall, Young, and Handsome?*

On New Year's Eve, 1982, as he dropped to one knee in the middle of Countryside Mall, I accepted his proposal, just four weeks from our first date. One stipulation … we need to be engaged for one year before the wedding.

The ring? It was an old diamond I had in my jewelry box. He had it set on a solid gold wide band. I loved it. Ha.

Uncle Frank and Aunt Sue were elated … and so was Scott!

24

Zitiello Family Values

Spring 1983

W HILE I WAS TRYING TO make sense of this situation, Scott and Tommy were building their own relationship. Scott's father was nowhere to be found, off sailing the Caribbean with his flavor of the month. Basketball, football, watching, and participating in sports—Tommy and Scott's common thread. Scott needed a male influence in his life. And they got along great. Tommy seemed to know just what to say to Scott and it warmed my heart to hear them in the garage talking about life.

Tommy's strong Catholic upbringing was something very important to me. He had a wild and crazy side, but he was anchored by his faith that was unwavering. The oldest of four children and the only son, his sisters worshipped him. They waited on him his entire life, and in return he watched out for them. When they got into any kind of trouble, he would help them out of it, trying hard to keep his parents from finding out. They had a very strong bond.

Tommy bragged that holidays, Catholic sacraments, showers, birthdays, and anniversaries were all celebrated in true Italian fashion. The ladies who made cakes and cookies for the First Holy Communion, did the same for all celebrations in the family. He was born and raised in Cleveland's Italian district, W64th, where the streets and the electric poles were painted with green, white, and red.

For over one hundred years, Cleveland's little Italy has celebrated the Feast of the Assumption, the celebration of Mary being taken into heaven. During this fall festival a statue of Mary with ribbons trailing from her head is carried through the streets. Faithful parish families would pin dollar bills to her ribbons as she passed by. You could literally smell the sauce cooking on the stoves, Tommy had said. His entire family attended each year.

He was proud of his Catholic faith, his Italian heritage, and the strong family bond and values they taught him. This was the single most important attribute that made me think a relationship with Tommy was possible. I longed for a strong family and traditions that could be counted on. Nothing more important could have prevented anyone in his family from missing any of these special occasions, nothing, a far cry from my dysfunctional family.

The winter cold had settled into Ohio with lake effect winds blowing freezing temperature and heavy snowstorms across the state. Cleveland takes the brunt of winter located on the shores of Lake Erie. The snowbirds flocked south. Tommy's family was no exception.

Between the two of us, we were enjoying the fruits of our labor with incentive checks and two salaries coming in. We were finally getting on our financial feet.

Tommy decided to rent a duplex in Dunedin, just a few miles away as soon as he heard his sisters and cousins planned to visit. He didn't want them to suspect we were living together. They were eager to meet the thirty-two-year-old divorcee with a twelve-year-old son who planned to marry their brother.

We sparsely equipped the place with blow-up mattresses, sheets and towels, a set of dishes, glasses, and pots and pans. There were ten of them coming and they viewed this trip to Florida like college spring break. Their wants were few—sun, beach, beer, and Hooter's chicken wings. We could easily manage to accommodate all of this.

When they arrived, we showed them their digs and they settled in quickly so they could get to the beach, start on their tans and those piña coladas from the beach hotel bar.

The steel drum bands could be heard down the white sugary stretch dotted with bright beach umbrellas. Tanned bodies laid on colorful beach towels as kiddies ran back and forth from the shore carefully carrying water in their buckets for the sandcastles that sprung up randomly. It was winter on Clearwater Beach.

They were a fun group excited to be on vacation away from the frosty north. It didn't take long to warm up to any of them. All three of the sisters were awesome. They each had distinct personalities and looks but shared a sarcastic sense of humor that left me smiling. The cousins were just the same. They were a fun-loving bunch who loved to party and that is exactly what we did.

They spent long days on the beach and bar-hopped at night. I felt completely accepted and while I had to work during the day, Scott and I managed to join them evenings for dinner and at the beach on the weekend. Even Uncle Frank and Aunt Sue and kids joined in to spend beach day with the family.

The week flew by quickly and it seemed just as I was getting to know them, they were flying back. They seemed to accept Scott and me willingly.

Tom continued to push for a wedding date, and hard as I tried, I couldn't get him to wait even one year. He wanted to make plans right away, but I was stalling. I loved him that was for certain, but I still felt it was too soon to say, "I do."

He had converted one of my bedrooms into an office. He hung the bar lights over his desk, arranged the handmade table with bright yellow pained chairs, and had cardboard legal boxes everywhere on the floor. I called it organized chaos. His presentations and products were everywhere.

Tommy spoke to his parents on the phone at least once a week. From the sound of it, the girls had gone back with a positive report. Now it was time for the parents to check out the potential newest members of the family. Plans were made for them to rent a condo at the golf course community nearby. While the underlying reason was meeting Scott and me, it was clearly a visit for the two brothers. Everyone was excited that Aunt Peggy and Uncle Lugi were coming for Easter week.

On my side of the family, things were much different. I spoke to my mom from my office about once a week, making sure to call her early because by afternoon she was too drunk to understand. She was so bitter about Dad and felt betrayed and abandoned. While I agreed completely, she had placed all three of her children smack dab in the middle of the two of them, and that was not right. We were forced to pick a side. Because Dad had visited me in Florida, she assumed I had chosen him over her. That too was not right. The phone call inevitably ended in tears and her shouting. Yet, I kept calling week after week.

Tom's parents were a breath of fresh air for me. They were loving and kind and fun to talk to. I wondered what they thought about divorce. Would they accept Scott too? Of course, I was a bit nervous, but I truly couldn't wait to meet them.

We had a great week together. They spent the days at Clearwater Beach or playing golf. Again, Tommy and I worked daily, Scott went to school. Evenings were always a planned dinner at a restaurant. Most of the time Frank and Sue and the kids were included. It was exactly what I had imagined, a large Italian family gathering around bowls of pasta and hands flying as crazy tales of the old neighborhood cascade off their lips.

There was one restaurant, Sue had discovered downtown Clearwater. "Ottavio's Place," very romantic and off the beaten path. The veal parmigiana was the best according to Lugi, and the fettuccini alfredo was like dessert. The attentive and very attractive maître d' sported a tux while his parents cooked each meal individually on the gas stove in the kitchen, a true family restaurant. There were only ten tables at that time.

"You discovered a winner, Sue," Tom's dad proclaimed and for future trips they would drive directly from the airport to *Ottavio's Place* upon arrival.

When it was time for the visit to come to an end, dinner plans were made for just the four of us. We settled in a booth and ordered our drinks. Tom's mom and dad sitting together across from the two of us.

Lugi shared his interest in Tom's job and warned him against messing it up. This was a reflection on Uncle Frank, so he better make good of it. We both assured him Tom was doing a great job. The conversation seemed different from the past days, more serious and reflective.

"Judi, I can see what is in this for Tommy, but what is in this for you?" he asked.

I spoke form my heart answering, "I love him."

"Well, I understand you want to have the wedding ceremony in Florida with your friends."

"Yes," we replied.

He suddenly glanced at his wife and nodded his head as his hands remained clasped on the table. She slowly reached into her purse and pulled out a cashier's check and handed it to him.

Lugi handed the check to me. "This is all he has," he announced. The check was for $3,200—his life savings.

"We would like to throw a reception for you in Cleveland the day after your wedding so everyone can meet you. Mommy and I will pay all expenses," he said.

Both of us looked at one another, me in disbelief, he with pride that his parents obviously approved and wanted to share our love with their family and friends.

I had passed the test. Tommy's parents had accepted both Scotty and me into their family. This was a huge sign that I must have made the right decision.

I was going to become a Zitiello. I needed God to help me with this decision. And for the first time ever, I prayed for God to show me that Tommy was the one for me.

25

The Job

THE EARLY SPRING BROUGHT SUCH promise when Tommy accepted a job offer with Clairol. He had to start at the bottom of the ladder, stocking shelves and doing "resets" at the retail grocery locations across his territory that carried the product line. His new boss Bill, a wonderful man, gave Tommy his first opportunity. Tommy had no college degree and no experience, but Bill saw the potential in this bright young man and after several interviews he was hired. My guy finally had a salary, company car, health insurance, and sales incentives. To say we were excited, including his Uncle Frank, is an understatement.

Large companies offer sales training to their account managers and Clairol was no exception. The first class that Tommy took was Dale Carnegies' "*How to Win Friends and Influence People.*" I don't believe he ever opened the book, but at the end of the course the attendees' vote for the person they feel will succeed in business. Of course, Tommy won the vote. I believe he possessed a natural ability to sell anything and anyone. After all, again, he had sold me!

He continued to wow his bosses, making large sales with his personal mantra of *"stack it high and let it fly."* Clairol had developed new scents for their popular Herbal Essence Shampoo. Tommy sold towering displays to health and beauty-aid buyers at grocery headquarter level, setting sales records that often frightened his boss who wondered if the product returns would outweigh this initial success. But Tommy was making a name for himself, yet he was eager to share his ideas with fellow account reps.

Tommy loved to include Scott and me in his sales promotions. Once he rented a twelve-foot sailboat and filled it with balloons and Sea Breeze Astringent in the health and beauty-aid section of the biggest grocery store in Clearwater. Tommy, Scotty, and I wore bright yellow Sea Breeze T-shirts and white shorts as we handed out cotton balls to customers.

Little old ladies couldn't resist Tommy as they accepted his sample saying, "Want a little zing in your life today? Try Sea Breeze."

"Nobody had ever thought to do such a thing," Bill commented. Tommy's territory sales were flying just as high as his displays and the truth was, he loved what he was doing.

He had finally found his niche.

Uncle Frank had paved the way, but Tommy had come through with flying colors. This former drywall hanger had traded his mud trowel in for a sales bag and he was headed to the top of the ladder.

I just knew he would be a huge success!

26

Wedding Number Three

IT WAS A GLORIOUS SPRING in Florida, six months since our first date. I had met his family and he had met my dad. Our relationship was moving quickly. Tommy continued to push to set a date and now it seemed even more important, he'd said. His parents would need to rent a hall and in Cleveland, dates filled up fast. While I felt a bit pressured, the romantic inside me was beaming.

There was no doubt in my mind I loved him. Our relationship so far was an enviable love story. I adored everything about him. While he was a wild and crazy, spontaneous guy, he had a soft and tender side that had captured my heart. And he made me laugh, something I hadn't done in a very long time. But, most importantly, he loved me with a deep and precious love. I felt completely safe for the first time in my entire life.

He had a bit of baggage to share with me. He explained about his baby son conceived in a six-week relationship. He believed because two people have a child together doesn't mean they must get married. He was financially responsible for his son and made sure each week a check was sent for his support. I admired this because my experience with estranged fathers was total abandonment. His loyalty to his son was another indication of a strong character.

I had taken a huge leap of faith with this partnership, and it seemed to have been the right thing to do. Well so far it had. I felt as if the Holy Spirit was holding my hand throughout this decision. And it felt right.

Twice I had divorced for unfaithfulness and physical and emotional abuse. Did my God condemn me for this? It seemed my church did. And how would the church view Tom with a son out of wedlock? This caused shame and guilt that was often overwhelming. Yet I believed in my heart that my God would not have judged us unfavorably for this; He would forgive us. Perhaps I was guilty of not seeking His discernment before I married either of the two weak men, and I would admit to that and confess countless times.

The Catholic church doesn't recognize a civil divorce and therefore will not allow the sacrament of marriage between two people unless the church dissolves the previous marriage through a lengthy and expensive process in the Vatican, an annulment.

Tommy didn't want to wait, and we both agreed we wanted the wedding ceremony in a church in front of a minister. My longtime friend and secretary belonged to a Methodist church and spoke to her pastor to see if he would perform the ceremony. He agreed and spoke to us about the process and questioned us both on our life expectations.

Both of us wanted our marriage blessed by God. We would have preferred to be married in the Catholic Church, but that just wasn't possible.

The pastor agreed to marry us on Friday August 4th in Clearwater. Tommy's parents found a hall and a band in Cleveland for the reception.

We would fly to Cleveland the morning after the Florida ceremony with Scott and our best man, Uncle Frank, and be introduced as Mr. & Mrs. Thomas Zitiello at our reception in the evening.

Tommy asked his Uncle Frank to be his best man and Scott to give me away. Both agreed instantly. We arranged a simple ceremony and invited a few neighbors, co-workers, and friends. I found a short lace dress that was perfect. Our plans were underway.

Then there was Tommy's question or the quiet assumption.

"We will invite your parents to the reception in Cleveland..."

The statement shook me back to a reality I had avoided, but it needed to be discussed. After all, our relationship was based on complete truth.

Tom had seen me on the phone with Mom on several occasions. I felt obligated to call her, but the late-night conversations of slurred words that inevitably ended up in conflict over what a poor husband Dad was were more than I could handle. I never wanted to be placed in the middle of them; she insisted on proving how he had abandoned her and us for another woman. That was a topic I felt should have been left between the two of them. I was completely embarrassed at her behavior.

Mom was living with her sister Lil and as hostess at the bar. What seemed like the perfect situation for them both, would end up adding fuel to an already raging fire. Mom drank every day. I avoided hearing her stories of the wonderful friends she had made with the regulars who came to the bar to sit for hours each day. They really cared about her she would tell me, insinuating they cared more than I did.

"At least someone does," she would say.

Tom thought I should invite Mom down to get to know him before we were married. I was completely against the idea. He insisted and we send her a ticket to visit for a weekend. The first night she had had a few drinks and said to Tom, "Well how long do you think you will last, Tom? You know she's been married twice, don't you?"

Tom looked at me in disbelief as he rushed me out of the room knowing I was embarrassed in front of our family and friends.

"How could any mother make a statement like that about her daughter?" he said.

He was shocked and saddened. That night we sat in the hot-tub, and Mom shared all the ugly stories with Tom that I had spared him. I was filled with hatred for her. If she couldn't be happy, she was going to make sure I wasn't either. We sent her off on the plane at the end of the weekend relieved she was gone.

The wedding plans had to be agreed upon.

Mom and Dad just could not be in the same room without a conflict erupting. And I certainly didn't want that to happen. Dad had walked, well rolled away in his wheelchair, in his weakened condition. I wasn't sure what would happen, should they come face to face. I explained to Tommy I just could not have Mom at the wedding. Maybe Dad and of course my sister and brother-in-law who were just a short drive from Cleveland. My brother was in the navy in Hawaii so he would not be able to attend. My mother would not spoil our special day.

Phone calls were made, invitations were mailed, and plans came together for a wonderful celebration.

It didn't include my mother.

Wedding week went just as planned, sweet, simple, and filled with love. While our nuptials would not include our traditional wedding mass, a ceremony performed by a minister on an altar with Jesus on the cross above us felt official and reverent. There was a small gathering at our house afterward complete with cake and champagne. And, in the morning we traveled to Cleveland where his family had prepared a perfect celebration.

It was a typical Italian wedding reception. Tons of amazing food spread out on the buffet. The smell of garlic filled the hall. Family, friends, and life-long neighbors were introduced as they passed through the receiving line. Many of the people attending were the same people who came to Tommy's baptism, first holy communion, confirmation, and graduation. While they ate, my new father-in-law made a wedding toast of prayers for many years of happiness for us and hopefully some children.

A band played as everyone danced. His family, now our family, wrapped their arms around Scotty and me immediately. They were very welcoming to my dad and his "friend" and, of course, my sister and brother-in-law. The only ones missing were Mom, my brother and sister-in-law who were stationed with the navy in Hawaii and could not attend. This was a dream come true, one I had lived through before.

Yet, this time it seemed different.

Tommy stood at the bar with his childhood friends passing shots and making toasts. Everyone was having a great time happy to be together again for such a joyous occasion.

We kissed Scott goodbye, leaving him with his new family as we left for a Caribbean cruise. His new aunts and cousins planned to take him to Cedar Point for a few days and one aunt would fly home with him at the end of the week. I felt comfortable about this and excited for Tommy and me to have a real honeymoon together.

It was official, I was now *"Mrs. Tall, Young, and Handsome."*

27

The Honeymoon Years

SETTLING INTO OUR LIFE TOGETHER was seamless. Tommy worked from home so he was there most afternoons when Scott would arrive from school. He loved to prepare dinner and he kept the house in order so I wouldn't stress when I finally came walking through the door after a long day at the office.

We were so in love. I couldn't wait to get home to my happy life. Everyone who knew us seemed to live through us in this great love story. Scott was thriving too.

Tommy and I had discussed having children at great length. He wanted a complete baseball team. For many years I had longed to have more children, and thank God, in His wisdom, hadn't granted this desire of my heart. But, at thirty-three my biological clock was ticking. We both knew we shouldn't wait too long.

Our happy life rocked on and two and a half years later, I shared with Tommy I was pregnant. We were elated. The doctor declared it to be a high-risk pregnancy because I was thirty-five. He assured us they would keep a good eye on me and there were tests that could be done to determine the baby was forming perfectly.

While we agreed we would not abort the pregnancy should the amniocentesis reveal an extra chromosome or anything seriously wrong with the development of our baby, we did have the procedure performed. We felt we could prepare if there was something wrong. One of the positives about the procedure was that it would reveal the sex of the child.

Naturally, Tommy wanted a son. He and his nephew Dominic were the only boys in his family to carry on the Zitiello name. So, not only did he want a little buddy to rock his sports teams, teach him to play ball and golf, but a gift to his parents whom he knew beyond a doubt would love and adore his child. That was just the kind of family who had raised him.

I couldn't wait to give him and them this gift, boy or girl.

28

Best News Ever

H<small>APPY DAYS TURNED INTO WEEKS</small> and months and life was full. I felt loved, safe, and secure with my husband and an exemplary model for my son who himself was growing a loving relationship with his stepfather.

My stressful life as a single working mother was transforming. While my career was at its height, the hours and travel required to continue to reach my business objectives often infringed on my happy life.

The business that had provided for our needs for eighteen years of my life was never one I would have chosen. My parents had never asked me what I was interested in or encouraged me to continue my education beyond high school.

Nobody had ever told me I could be anything I wanted to be, or that my dreams were unlimited.

My dad, a successful executive with a large heavy equipment dealership that covered the entire state; my mom, a stay-at-home mom. Her job was to raise the children and take care of the familial home. Dad had continued his education, but it wasn't necessary for Mom to stay in school when at seventeen Dad told her to quit cosmetology school. And Mom had never heard the statement she could be anything she wanted to be or that her dreams were reachable. It was a different time, a time when the role of woman was simply wife and mother.

Well, in my world that was the case.

I was super successful at my job and received financial compensation that ranked me in the top percent of women in the nation. Up to this point it was the only positive recognition I received. It had kept me running that treadmill with no time to look back to question my career choice. So, who was complaining?

I had never been one to look back and feel remorse. I knew vividly the mistakes I had made and suffered the consequences of them. I was proud to have risen above it all and hopefully been a good mom all the while. It seemed foolish to think of the "what ifs." I was indeed a survivor.

Now my life was taking a dramatic turn, one that was unfamiliar to me. I was placing my trust in my husband, and while it felt good, that old worry crept into my mind often. It truly seemed too good to be true.

A few months after our wedding Dad decided to move to Florida to escape the brutal winters forcing him to stay tucked inside. Of course, he would be bringing his friend along. Sooner or later, I would need to accept her … the woman who stole my father away from not just my mother … my sister and brother and me. I wasn't sure if I could do that.

But, once again, my sweet Tommy in his youthful innocence and forgiving spirit showed me that I should be thanking this woman who was taking great care of my disabled dad. He was right of course. I was walking on unfamiliar paths. I was learning how to be the woman he knew I was. Funny, I hardly knew her myself.

The day came when I proudly shared with my employer, we were going to have a baby. What would happen to my job was no longer a concern.

Tommy told me "Don't worry, we will work it all out. The most important thing was we are having a baby."

29

Good News, Bad News

A FEW MONTHS LATER I TOOK a call from my secretary while I was on a trip to Atlanta. She told me the results were in from the amniocentesis and I should call my OB-GYN right away. She tracked Tommy down at a grocery store where he was working a retail reset and phoned me with his number while I spoke to the doctor's office. (No mobile phones back then!) Someone announced over the PA a call for Tommy Zitiello.

When we finally were connected, I shared the news.

"It's a boy and he is developing fine—no abnormalities," I shouted with excitement.

I could hear his happiness and relief come right through the phone as he replied, "You do everything just perfectly."

We were having a boy and his name would be Louis John Zitiello. It was truly not up for discussion. For generations his family had named the firstborn son Louis John. The firstborn son of Louis John was named Thomas Louis. I loved the tradition of it. I loved the strong expectation that this would be carried on for generations into the future, our future, and now the future of our child. It was more than just a name to us now. As we announced our good news to the family near and far, everyone was elated.

This news was overshadowed by some developments just a few months before. Tommy's Uncle Frank, thirty-six years old, had been diagnosed with pancreatic cancer. They thought it might have been something he had carried home from his stint in the service overseas in Korea. He was struggling physically but fighting hard.

We spent many hours at his hospital bedside giving his wife Sue a break. Their children were young, so we all took shifts where we could to help. When he was released from the hospital, we continued to help, but the prognosis was not good. We felt blessed to have the chance to tell him about our baby boy and he reacted with that beautiful wide smile, weak as he was.

This was Tommy's dad's brother, the youngest of three, two boys and a girl. And the person responsible for bringing Tommy and me together.

They were an incredibly close family, and this was difficult to swallow since both parents, Tommy's grandparents, had passed away just a few years before. Tom's dad and mother had visited once during his illness and Frank had made a trip to Cleveland for his sister's anniversary party. Sadly, he passed a few months after that and a few months before little Louis arrived.

We found ourselves in church once again, surrounded by family and friends. On this solemn occasion, we were weeping rather than rejoicing. Frank was buried in the family plot purchased in the early 1900s when Frank's Grandfather Luigi (Louis) Zitiello, like so many others, had entered through Ellis Island from Caserta, Italy.

At the cemetery, a large marble statue of an angel with the Zitiello name carved into the stone stood surrounded by a black iron fence where his grave was prepared. He would rest for eternity next to his grandparents, and eventually, other members of his family.

The same ladies brought the same dishes for the buffet at the wake where music played, and the strong smell of freshly brewed coffee filled the air. They assembled once again to celebrate a life of one of their own.

This was now my heritage too. And I loved it.

30

Scott's Big Request

THE HOLIDAYS WERE FAST APPROACHING, and my due date, close to Thanksgiving. It was football season for Scott, and we didn't miss a game.

Under his new dad's tutorage, Scott had developed into an amazing athlete. The evening workouts in our garage had paid off. The weight bench and pull up bar had really bulked him up. He was a formidable linebacker on his high school offensive team playing varsity and starting while he was only a freshman.

His faith was developing too. Years of CCD were paying off. He was a sensitive young man who never caused us any worry. His behavior was exemplary.

Reading and math were huge challenges for him considering his dyslexia. He handled this all with grace and patience. His teachers loved him. He tried hard to make up for his academic shortcomings and he was succeeding. The label he had to wear would carry him through life being big-hearted and strong.

A few weeks before Scott's fifteenth birthday we shared with him we would be having a baby in the fall. When I asked him what he wanted for his birthday, I was thrilled with his response. He explained how he wanted to be adopted by Tom. When his brother was born, we would all share the same name. Tom was equally as happy about the idea. We contacted an attorney to begin the process right away.

Since Scott's adoptive father had not truly assumed the official role, we thought there would be no issue with him signing the papers that would allow the adoption.

Then there was the matter of over $20,000 in child support arrearage with the court. We knew we could leverage that as a bargaining chip.

When it came time for the final paperwork to be signed, Scott had to release his father from the obligation of the back support. I took him into his bedroom and sat beside him with the paper in my hand.

I had never been one to speak badly about his father. God knows, his actions spoke louder than any words I could impart. I felt it was important to make him understand what was happening.

"Scott, when you sign this document, you are telling the court that your father does not need to pay you the $20,000 he owes you in child support. I want you to know this because if he ever makes you feel as if you owe him something ... you do not."

He looked serious as I asked him if he understood. He shook his head affirmatively and said, "Yes."

We never spoke about that ever again.

The papers were given to the court and the adoption was granted. He now was a Zitiello too, and very proud of it. On his fifteenth birthday, we presented him with a dark-burgundy-colored varsity jacket, his varsity letter attached, and his name, "Scott Zitiello" embroidered over his heart.

"Welcome to the family," Tommy announced.

The girls noticed Scott right away with his good looks and athletic stature. When other football players showed up in the garage for a workout, you could be assured several cheerleaders would follow. Tom enjoyed mentoring the kids and they loved him too. After all he was just twelve years older and was passionate about sports. He was still a kid at heart too.

It was a far cry from the solitude that Scott and I had lived for a few years. And we both took immense pleasure in the change.

31

Welcome to the World, Little One

WE WERE ENERGIZED AT THE thought of welcoming a new member of the family as we painted the small sitting room next to the master bedroom light blue and pasted the teddy bear border around the perimeter of the room. We prepared for the arrival of our new son.

Tom's mother and father were scheduled to visit for two weeks in late November. We would be together for Thanksgiving and hopefully the baby would arrive too. It was a good time for the visit because Sue and the kids were still reeling from the loss of Frank. Dominic was just twelve years old and Lisa was fifteen. Tom and I made sure to include them in family meals and football games as often as possible. And seeing Uncle Lugi and Aunt Peggy would be a great boost for them.

A visit from his parents was always fun, long meals at great restaurants, lazy days on the warm white sands of Clearwater beach sipping piña coladas while the sounds of a steel drum band playing at the hotel pool floated on the ocean breeze. They were always up for a game of liar's poker or a run to the casino at the Tampa Indian Reservation for some all-night Bingo. It was something we all looked forward to.

Scott soaked up the attention too. They never missed a football game when they visited. They would sit with us on the bleachers, cheering the Tarpons Spongers on to victory as Scott ran the field. His HS team was amazing, so it was fun for this family of sports enthusiasts.

Sunday morning, we would not miss mass, but two more Zitiellos would be sitting in our pew, then off to the regular Sunday morning breakfast joint where we would make our plans for the rest of the day.

Everyone anticipated the arrival of little Louis John, but Thanksgiving came and went, and their visit was ending and nothing had happened. They would be leaving on Saturday morning.

Friday night, the guys went to the football game, but my mother-in-law and I remained at home because I didn't feel just right. I was having what I thought were Braxton-Hicks—pre labor pains as I had off and on for several days. But, late that evening, we drove to the hospital and the next morning, as the plane carried Grandma and Grandpa back to Cleveland, he arrived.

My labor was long and hard and after too many hours the doctor suggested a C-section. Tommy and the doctor both entered the labor room to ask my consent. I was thankful to agree. They wheeled me into the delivery room. I would be holding my little angel shortly.

After prepping me and draping me, our view into the large mirror above was the window we shared as he entered the world.

When he took his first breath and let out a healthy cry, Tommy and I cried too. They laid his little pink body on my belly as they cut the cord and sewed me back up. It was one of the happiest moments of our lives together.

As I held my little guy against my skin, I noticed that unmistakable new baby smell, fresh and pure and full of life. He was a product of our love for one another … in the form of a human being. God had given us both an amazing gift and our hearts were exploding with love.

Tom called his parents to share all the details and to make plans for when we would get together. He also called my dad to give him the news. They were thrilled.

At that moment I wondered how anyone could question the existence of God. We had witnessed a miracle as clearly as any I had ever seen. We were complete.

The nursery was awaiting our little angel, his wooden crib and dresser the beautiful sheets, bumpers, and quilts, quite a contrast from Scotty's arrival in the middle of a military discharge and travel back to Michigan. Little Louis had it all.

When we were discharged, we drove home, placing our angel in his blue bassinet in the family room as a parade of family and friends came to meet the newest little Zitiello.

Maternity leave would last for six weeks, and I was delighted to be home full time. I decided to breast feed him and that worked out well for us. He was thriving. I enjoyed being a full-time wife, mother, and housewife for those six weeks.

I knew I had to return to work, so we interviewed until we found the perfect nanny for little Louis. Lilly was in her mid-fifties and Italian. In fact, she didn't speak much English at all. She had been recommended by the maître d' at our favorite restaurant *Ottavio's*, a family friend. She seemed perfect. We hired her and I headed back to work truly not happy but, I put on my suit and heels, a smile, and off I went, ready to jump back into corporate America.

We never missed mass, the three of us, and now we were four sitting in our pew near the back of the church just in case Louis needed to be rushed to the cry room.

We met with the priest to plan Louis' baptism. It was important to get this done as soon as he was six weeks old, recalling something deep within me that echoed this command. And we did.

I was really beginning to feel a transformation coming over me. I thanked God for His blessings and prayed they would never be taken away.

While I felt unworthy, I knew He must have seen my tears all those many years. What had I done to deserve His grace in my life? It was almost overwhelming.

God had found a place in my heart, and I wasn't going to let Him slip away.

32

A Big Surprise!

IT WAS STRANGE THAT THE career that had once been my number one priority now seemed to have slipped to a low third or fourth on my list. I had changed. My life had changed. Most importantly my happiness level had jumped to a whopping 10!

Tom's dad was having a big birthday the end of January. The weather was bitter cold and snowing when we landed at Cleveland Hopkins Airport. We planned to surprise him with an unannounced visit and gift him with his newest grandson named after him, as was the tradition.

We stood next to a payphone just outside *Ferris' Steakhouse* where the family had gathered to celebrate Dad's fiftieth. Snowflakes the size of dinner plates drifted to the already snow-covered sidewalk.

"Sorry we can't make it up there, Dad." I heard Tom say. "It's just the baby is too small to travel."

He knew his dad would agree. He wished him a happy birthday and told him we would see them as soon as we could.

Minutes later we entered the restaurant and presented him his namesake donned in a white onesie on which we had printed "*Happy 50th Birthday Grandpa Lugi*." He appeared surprised, but today I wonder if he truly was. I had learned there was not much that slipped past this wonderful man.

The rest of the family gathered at their house the next day to meet little Louis. It was official, the name would continue.

It was a short trip because I had just started back to work. We returned to Florida and happily looked forward to the Easter visit with his sisters and parents just weeks ahead.

Tom made it clear I should try to get home from work at a reasonable hour so we could have dinner with Scott, feed and bathe the baby together. While I wanted to make this happen, it was easier said than done. I promptly got up from my desk at 5:30 PM each day, well most days.

Working in financial services is a highly competitive career based on sales quotas. The slate was wiped clean on the first of each month, and as the month progressed, the objectives predicted the hours spent to achieve them. Being responsible for seven offices required travel too. I covered the West Coast of Florida and made scheduled visits. I reported to the Atlanta division office and would be asked to fly up for meetings there as well. These were difficult trips away from Tommy and my two boys.

Toms' career was just beginning to take off. I knew he was a natural salesman, and the proof was there for all to see. The first year with this national health and beauty aid company, he broke all records, landing their highest sales award. The headhunters began to call. He wasn't looking for a job. He was happy with Clairol, and they promised the next position he was dreaming of. However, he would listen to the propositions, flattered by the attention.

Just one week after I returned to work from maternity leave, I was called to Atlanta for an emergency meeting. I took the earliest plane out of Tampa to arrive in time for the 8 AM meeting. I wore a red suit and carried my briefcase and purse. No need for a suitcase as I planned to catch a late flight back to Tampa.

When I exited the plane, I felt strange. I headed for the ladies-room to discover something was terribly wrong. I was bleeding heavily; my skirt was soaked in blood. I washed and dried my skirt with the hand air dryer. I wasn't alarmed, I hadn't gotten my period because I had been nursing. But since I had returned to work, I wasn't producing much milk and not pumping regularly. I figured this was normal. I was just getting back into my cycle. I planned to call my doctor as soon as I got to the office. When I did, he ordered me to get back as soon as I could and come to his office the next day.

My work meeting was extremely stressful, a chewing out of all the AVPs about disappointing results. We were sent back with a renewed purpose created by the firing of one of our own. This was not what I needed, but of course I had not shared with my bosses, all male, what was going on with me, not wanting to appear a weak woman.

The next morning, I lay on the doctors' table being examined.

"Hmmm" he said, "something is not right here."

He ordered a test and I moved to the next office and prepared for the sonogram.

"Here is sack A and here is sack B," reported the tech performing the sonogram.

"What sacks are you referring to?" I asked quizzically.

"You are pregnant ... and with twins." She smiled as the words fell from her lips like musical notes.

Then her smile turned to concern. "Sack B doesn't look just right. I can't find the heartbeat."

The doctor explained I was indeed pregnant and sack B was a "blighted ovum," not a viable fetus. While sack A was thriving with a strong heartbeat, my body would probably expel both sacks as a natural miscarriage.

His instructions, it was okay to continue to work, call him when the miscarriage takes place, and he would arrange a D&C. It all seemed so clinical. My mind was spinning.

I called Tom to explain what had happened. With each sentence he went from joy to sorrow. He was thrilled with the idea of me being pregnant ... and with twins! WOW. But as I explained what the doctor had told me, we agreed to keep this to ourselves until the miscarriage occurred. This was our first storm together.

He assured me we would weather it together and we would pray about it. And, each Sunday, we sat in our special pew and prayed for this little baby that was growing each day. Sadly, we anticipated the day when it would grow no more.

Weeks passed and nothing happened except my almost flat belly had returned to a bump. The doctor had said if I carried the baby five months, chances were, I would deliver. That five-month objective seemed to take years. We focused on our little Louis to keep our spirits up. He was perfect and funny and filled our evenings and weekends with complete and utter joy. He was adorable and the perfect distraction.

At my five-month check, the doctor ordered an amniocentesis.

"I guess you are going to have this baby," he said.

This time we felt it was important to determine if the baby had any medical issues we needed to prepare for. It was better than being anxious for the entire pregnancy for sure. So, we proceeded with the test that would take a full month for the results.

Once we reached the fifth month of the pregnancy, there was no way to hide it. We agreed it was time to announce to my employer I was pregnant again. I was extremely apprehensive. Management handled the first six-week maternity leave quite well. They had arranged for a temporary replacement. It allowed them to put a promising AVP into the position without a commitment. But how would they react to this news happening less than a year later?

I requested the meeting and was again surprised at their positive reaction. Well, maybe it was that they had already figured it out.

Louis wasn't even walking yet, and my belly was growing fast; as the months passed, it was difficult for me to pick him up. At ten months he was walking. The little guy was forced to grow up quickly and he seemed not to mind one bit. He was loved, as was the little angel in my belly.

The results were in. The baby was developing perfectly. Then the best news ever ... it was a girl! I had secretly dreamed of a girl with each of my previous pregnancies. Now my dream would come true.

I was happy to give Tommy the boy he also dreamed of when Louis came along, now that pressure was off.

I could finally have a soft pink bundle that would one day grow into my best friend. God was so good to have granted me my dream. I was relieved she was thriving and healthy.

I remember thanking God at church that Sunday with tears spilling down my cheeks as I stared at the big wooden cross above the altar where Jesus hung. Tommy and I felt our prayers were answered. I was filled with gratitude.

Scott was growing up so fast. He was the best big brother ever. He continued to work out with Tom in the garage gym they had put together. The Tarpon Spongers were a formidable team, making it to states two years in a row. Several of his football teammates would join Tommy and Scott for nightly workouts after practice in our garage gym. He was a great kid and had friends we more than approved of.

That was another thing I was thankful for. There were many reasons Scott could have, maybe even should have gone the other way. He had never known his biological father. He had lived with an emotionally abusive stepfather. My career kept me working many hours, sometimes weekends. He had needed a supportive and nurturing male figure in his life.

I was so glad that he and Tommy were growing closer and closer. He finally had a father figure he could respect and admire. That was another huge blessing from this unconventional union.

Before each football game, Scott would stop at our church with one or two teammates, to say a prayer for all of the players to be safe and for them to play a good and fair game. Then, before they took the field, the entire team would take a knee. His faith was growing just as quickly as his body, and I loved what I saw.

The date was made for my scheduled C-section. November 10th was the date. She would arrive just 11 months and 10 days after Louis! We would celebrate his first birthday a couple of weeks after the birth.

I often thought during those last weeks had the twin survived we would have had three babies all under one year old! Now that would have been crazy! We would have embraced it somehow and made it through it.

We prepared the nursery for a second crib and dresser, two babies in diapers, two car seats, two of everything. It was going to be challenging. But we were excited and happy to tackle it.

Lilly was working out great with Louis and welcomed another baby to care for. We loved the fact she would speak Italian to the babies and who knows, maybe some words would stick. It was a relief to have someone at the house all day with no other responsibilities than the babies.

The birth would be completely different from Louis'. Grandma and Grandpa Lugi arrived from Cleveland in plenty of time. They took Louis to the beach while we headed to the hospital. I was scheduled for an 8 AM delivery. I showered, applied my makeup, blew my hair dry. It seemed funny thinking by 8:15 AM, I would be holding my little baby girl!

That is pretty much what happened. The birth went as planned and within a few minutes I was holding my sweet angel. She was soft and pink and had just a little hint of light brown hair. She was perfect. It was all just as I had imagined except nobody mentioned I would have labor pains post-op. While Tommy and his family played with my little bundle, I was in pain. Every pain was worth it. Even Louis was excited to meet his little sister.

We named her Lindsay.

For several years, Uncle Cal and Aunt Ethel would invite us to their rustic log cottage on the banks of Lake Huron on the Canadian side. It was always such fun on the lake swimming and boating with cousins. Aunt "Et" had some college-age nieces and nephews who visited too. They had a convertible sports car and the handsome guys took us tweens for a ride up and down the dirt roads leading to the cottage. I remember watching how they enjoyed the lake, tanned and beautiful, especially the girl named Lindsay. I never forgot the name and now I had chosen it for my little girl with dreams of her growing beautiful, sun-kissed, and happy. Lindsay was also the character starring in a current television show *The Bionic Woman*. Our little star had battled so much to make it to this point, she deserved a strong name.

Uncle Cal and Aunt Et sent her first nosegay of pink baby roses and a white tulle with trailing pale pink ribbons. It was so thoughtful, and I appreciated the gesture so much.

Lugi and Peggy, Dad and his second wife Dolores, Scott and his girlfriend Blake came to the hospital to visit. Even my mom and Bob, now husband number two, paid us a visit. (Of course, we had to give them time frames so there was no drama.) They were all there to share in our happiness.

A few days later, we brought her home. I looked forward to having our favorite time of year, the entire holiday Thanksgiving to Christmas and New-Years off from work with my growing family.

Life was perfect. I began to wonder if I could ever be happier.

33

Our Beautiful Life

W E SAILED THROUGH THE NEXT couple of years as both of our careers continued to soar. Tommy was working with a large national drug company calling on Kmart at the headquarter level as a Key Account Manager. He continued to shine by breaking every sales goal wide open and winning every incentive program they put in front of him.

When I returned to work after my second maternity leave, they offered me a promotion to Training Department AVP responsible for developing the training programs for our newly formed mortgage company. It was a big job, but it gave me the opportunity to exercise my creative side through developing a company newspaper, job-specific training programs, and weeklong sales seminars for employees at all levels. I loved it.

I worked out of the Tampa Division office and there was just a bit of travel. This balanced out well with Tom's more intense travel schedule. Scotty and his girlfriend, both now in high school, were able to fill in as babysitters when it became necessary. But we managed to seldom be away from the babies at the same time.

Headhunters and agencies were constantly approaching Tommy with offers, but while he had no desire to change jobs, he would always listen. We agreed he would ask for the moon and if they would offer him the moon and the stars, he would seriously consider the opportunity to move on.

One day he came to me with an offer he had been considering. This one was different than most. If we accepted, he would be joining a small brokerage as a manufacturer's rep, selling health and beauty aids and housewares to retail grocery and drug chain headquarters in the southeast, an agency run by a longtime family friend. Previously the president of the agency and Tom's Uncle Frank had worked together at a larger brokerage. We knew this dynamic Greek very well and were always treated like family when we were together. If Uncle Frank was invited, so were we. The friends dreamed of putting together their own company one day.

Fate had turned a blind eye to this plan when Tom's Uncle died of pancreas cancer at thirty-six just two years before. This guy said he would like to have the next-best person join him, Frankie's nephew … Tommy.

This was a big opportunity but along with it came huge risk. This was pretty much a startup company that had been in business just a few years. He would be giving up the security a big corporation offered, but it would also provide unlimited income potential.

Of course, he was flattered, but a total commission sales rep with limited benefits would not be enough to tempt him to leave the great employment package and expense account he had with a national company. He was confident he could sell, but it would cost him plenty to make the move. He would have to buy a car, pay for insurance, and would never know what his monthly income would be. It was just not an offer he could consider as a new father and husband. He would need more plus a percentage of ownership in the company.

Our friend was serious and obviously saw the potential in Tommy. So, a new proposal included twenty percent ownership and an attractive draw. He would be given a large account with built-in business—but it would require us to move to Jacksonville.

We had to make some quick decisions. The Jacksonville account was a four-hour drive and to be effective, he would need to camp out there all week. Would we want to split up our family life for this very dubious opportunity?

Part of me wanted to be the stay-at-home mom Tommy wanted me to be, but I had to consider giving up my dream job. I had to take another huge leap of faith in my husband. Plus, the financial uncertainty was difficult to accept.

Tommy was a proven salesman. I had to show him that I truly believed in him. I could tell this was what he wanted to do. So, I told him it made sense if he took this chance now, while I had the income to cover the bills and great benefits. He could travel as he needed to. It really was no different than what we had been doing for the past two years anyway. We would see how it went and if it all panned out, we would consider moving to Jacksonville in the future.

God intervened quickly. News came that Michael, the company president, had been diagnosed with lung cancer. He traveled to Sloan Kettering for surgery and treatment. He asked Tommy to remain local to run the office while he battled his diagnosis, so no move to Jacksonville would be required for an undetermined time.

While we prayed for Michael to beat his cancer, we realized Tommy was given the opportunity to learn the management and administration aspect of the business. It was a bit different from working for a manufacturer and selling just one list of products. Now he had over two hundred lines to sell. He needed to learn everything about each line while he developed his relationships with vendors and buyers of the food and drug chains in the southeast. He was a quick study, but God really gave him this time to grow and learn and expand his circle of contacts within this niche business known as Health and Beauty-Aids and Housewares/General Merchandise. It was working to everyone's advantage.

There was another principal of the team who lived in South Florida who had worked with Uncle Frank. Bobby was a great guy with a huge personality. He had a wealth of experience and welcomed Tommy as a partner with open arms. In this unique business there was no need for competitive envy. If the company did well, all three partners shared in the profits. So … sell on everyone.

On the shirttail of his Uncle Frank, Tommy was developing relationships and a reputation that would carry him through many successful years.

The best part was he was passionate about what he was doing.

Each Sunday we attended mass at the Catholic church we called our parish home. We would sit in the third pew from the back of the church and sometimes in the cry room while the babies wriggled and climbed during mass. Afterward we would have brunch at a breakfast place, sometimes with neighbors and friends. It was great to give one hour each week to God to thank Him for all He had blessed us with.

We celebrated both babies' first sacrament, baptism, faithfully at six weeks of age again, surrounded by family and friends.

We would call on this place of peace and comfort in our lives many, many times in the years to come as we faced the trials that come to all of us. I was learning that trials would inevitably come. I was preparing for that shoe to fall as it had in the past, while praying it would not.

Life was too perfect.

34

Mr. and Mrs. Palm Harbor

SCOTT AND BLAKE WERE IN love. They had dated since Scott was a sophomore in high school. Scott played varsity football his sophomore year and junior year at the same school with Blake, a senior and captain of the varsity cheerleaders. His junior year, Blake's senior year, the football team made it to the state championship. While they lost in a "Hail Mary" pass in the last seconds of the game, it was an exciting year for all of us.

Blake was beautiful! She had a strong will and was a great student active in every club she could manage. She seemed not to be surprised by our crazy antics and even joined in. Best of all, she loved our Scotty.

Our son hadn't really dated around. He was serious about Blake and football in that order. She would eventually go on to Florida State while he finished his senior year. Then he went on to Arizona Western for summer session and one fall semester.

He came home from AW at Christmas and never returned. It was just too isolated there and he missed Blake and his family. He enrolled at the local community college and lived at home.

Tommy and I did everything we could to help them realize they should date others to make sure their love was the real thing. We felt it was the sensible thing to do.

They remained true and Christmas Eve two years later, before Blake graduated college, Scott proposed, after properly asking for her hand. It came as no surprise to anyone as we clicked the champagne glasses in celebration surrounded by family. They planned a long engagement, a spring wedding more than a year away. Thankfully that allowed Scott to get his schooling and job secured before they would begin their life together as Mr. and Mrs. Scott Zitiello.

35

Mom Update

MOM, THE SURVIVOR SHE HAD become, found security in marrying Bob just a few months after meeting him at happy hour at a nearby Florida restaurant on her first trip to visit us.

I found it odd Mom would want to leave us during a weekend visit to go off somewhere with our neighbor when she was clearly only with us for a few short days! Our neighbor who had become one of Mom's close friends since Mom had moved in with me early in my separation from number two, invited her out for the evening.

And that is how she met Bob.

Bob had lost his wife some time ago and would frequent a local restaurant for appetizers and drinks and to listen to the band. All the seniors on the prowl hung out here, so of course, my neighbor took Mom there the weekend she visited us. When she returned to Michigan, they stayed in contact.

One week later she called me early in the morning. As I answered she greeted me with a chipper "Good morning … guess where I am?"

I truly had no clue where this conversation was leading.

"I'm back in Florida, I've moved in with Bob."

Bob had survived numerous heart bypass surgeries and was not in good health. He fell instantly in love with her and asked her to move in with him in his modest ranch home just a few miles from the beach. His twenty-something son and daughter who lived nearby grieved for their mother yet seemed to accept Mom with little reservation, or at least that was what I understood to be true.

In a short time, Bob and Mom eloped. She was on to husband number two.

Within a few weeks, she had completely re-landscaped his yard and added her own decorating touches to make the little home hers. In a few months, she took him condo shopping and a for-sale sign went up on Bob's free and clear house. It sold at once.

Mom and Bob moved into the newly constructed two-bedroom condo she had selected. It wasn't long before she had created a tropical garden complete with thatched roof and a small Koi-pond in the tiny backyard. They loved to sit and enjoy endless cocktails.

The yard was surrounded with a tall pine fence that blocked out the noise and neighbors. They added a double-door gate that could be opened to the corner. They had a little Yorkie who ran the household.

Mom was a survivor and was happy so long as she had her home, her dog, and her garden. She never admitted to loving Bob, but she knew he would provide for her and that made it all worthwhile. She told me she looked at it as a job of sorts.

Within a few short years Bob's heart just couldn't keep up and he passed. He left the condo to Mom and some certificates of deposit. She would be able to remain independent for a while if she didn't go too crazy. He had prearranged and paid for his final plans. He was buried in a cemetery close to their home and there were just family and a few close friends in attendance.

I felt badly for Bob's children. They had lost both parents within a few years. And they were just young adults. Mom had not stepped in as their stepmother in any capacity. She really offered nothing more than her kindness should they reach out to her. Of course, their calls and visits stopped when Bob died.

Mom didn't even mark Bob's grave with a stone. She didn't see the need to honor someone in this way. It seemed selfish and cruel to me that someone who gave his heart to her, his bank account and put a roof over her head didn't deserve to leave a mark on this earth when he left.

She returned to her condo, her dog, and her comfortable life, having landed on her feet, like a cat, once again.

36

Dad Leaves for the Last Time

DAD AND HIS GIRLFRIEND OF now twenty-six years had moved to Florida to escape the harsh Michigan winters shortly after Tommy and I married. We had purchased an investment condo with Tommy's parents. Dad and Dolores moved in as our tenants.

It was a small two-bedroom condo on the ground floor. Dad had no difficulty getting his large wheelchair in and out. It had a small, screened porch where Dolores grew orchids and Dad could sit and watch the pond just beyond the sidewalk. He loved the wildlife and had embraced the Florida bird and alligator population as they sunned on the bank each day. Florida life was a great alternative.

Dolores was a great cook and while it was difficult for me to accept her, she did take very good care of Dad as Tom would often remind me. They would drive the short distance from the condo to our house for visits on Sundays after church to see the babies. Dolores would make her famous cherry-chocolate cake that everyone loved. (Actually, my sister Sherrie's recipe.)

Dad and Dolores were married in the same church that Tom and I had married in a few months previously. I was happy for Dad, but still held deep resentment for Dolores for having turned my entire life upside down and hurting my mother. I tried to tuck those feelings away and be the better person I knew Tom wanted me to be.

Having my parents live so close by might sound like a good thing in most cases. But in this instance, it was difficult. Mom had never gotten over Dad. She still loved him deeply. She would drink each afternoon and phone me. She again accused me of choosing sides with Dad. It was difficult being in the middle of this perpetual argument and was the basis for me escaping to Florida in the first place.

And now, they all had followed me here.

Tommy, always the voice of reason, could never understand how any family could not forgive and forget and place the children before themselves. I had never known the security he felt with his mother and father. They truly had unconditional love for their children. That was the kind of love I had for Scott and the kind of love I would have for our children now. We would break this chain of dysfunction together.

Sitting in church each Sunday I noticed the same families, week after week, month after month and year after year. We watched as young families grew. There was truth in the statement *"families who prayed together stayed together."* This was what I wanted for our life. And I was willing to fight for it, whatever it took.

But wanting something and truly changing the scripts in our minds that run over and over again of our memories from the past requires real effort. Our love was strong, but life constantly throws us challenges and temptations from a world that doesn't hold the same beliefs and morals we fight to live by.

My life had been one of "if he hurts me, I will hurt him back." I knew this justification was completely wrong and I was fighting to change the almost immediate gut reactions I had repeated. Those reactions had proven unsuccessful twice before. I wasn't going to let it happen a third time.

I was determined to allow the love Tom showed me to take over my heart. He had been truthful, the first person in my life to never tell me a lie. While I was still skeptical, I was committed. I loved him more than anything in the world, and he had proven he would give me my hearts – desire.

When I would try to explain my hesitation, he would remind me not to paint him with the same brush stroke … he deserved a chance to show me he was nothing like them.

And so far, he was right.

Life continued happily with our routine of working all week and looking forward to weekends with the kids.

Some Saturday mornings Tom would wake up and say, "OK today we are going to Busch Gardens."

We never did anything without including the children. They loved it, and so did we. Every Sunday we sat in mass giving God our thanks for bringing our little family together as our love story continued.

Then, the day we had seen approaching finally did. We got a call from Dad's doctor. He had been admitted to the hospital and he told us we needed to contact family members and get them there as soon as we could. I phoned Sherrie in Arizona and Ernie in California and told them the news. They never made it to his side.

His wife had been sitting continuously by his side for three days. We visited daily after work. And one afternoon I suggested she go get some rest and take a break.

Dad's breathing was shallow. He was in and out of consciousness. I held his hand and spoke softly to him, rambling on about fun times together. I wondered if he knew Jesus and if he had prepared himself for death. He had been given ten years since his stroke and I guessed he had faced the thought of death many times. But had he really asked God's forgiveness and accepted Jesus as his personal savior? I didn't have the courage to ask him before, but now I needed to know. I told him we would all be together in heaven one day assuming he had thought about that. I never really got a firm confirmation. I had to accept that was between Dad and God. I prayed he was ready.

Surprised when the nurse came in and told me he would soon pass, I held his hand tightly. I cried as I encouraged him it was ok to let go. I realized I might be hurting his hand I was squeezing it so tightly. He was moving his hand as if trying to tell me something and then he released a deep breath and he was gone.

I sat for a long time thinking about this moment. Dad had been there when I entered this world and now, I had sat holding his hand as he departed.

My Dad had left us, and this time he was gone for good.

37

Life is Grand!

1993

B LAKE GRADUATED FROM FSU AND moved back home with her mom and took a job in retail while she waited to snag a position with the school system as a teacher. Scott continued to work two jobs and take a class here and there. They set a date close to Valentine's Day and we began to plan their wedding.

We held a meeting with Blake and her mom, Scott, Tom, and me to discuss the wedding details. She would have her dress made and most of the detail work on it she would do herself. Her mom was willing to do whatever she could to help with the limited financial resources she had.

It was important to Tom to make this wedding an event to remember. It was one of the sacraments of our faith and it was going to be marked with a proper amount of celebration.

The snowball left the top of the mountain and it rolled on and on.

By the time it landed, we had planned a one-week celebration including some activity or party each day.

Tom was determined to make the trip from Ohio to Florida eventful for his relatives and the many clients and friends he had met through business for the past five years.

We set the date with our church and met with the priest, the bride, and groom to complete pre-marital classes.

The new country club just a mile from our house was perfect for our reception and pre-wedding rounds of golf. We reserved a dozen rooms at a convenient hotel and an extra room to be used as a meeting place for our guests and friends complete with beer and snacks, card tables for poker just steps from the hotel pool. It was perfect.

Wedding week went off without a hitch, and the parties were truly epic. I had never been to any wedding like this in my life, nor had anyone else. Tom certainly had a vision of how to throw a party.

So many memories of the reception! The song choice they had made for the mother–son dance left everyone in tears, "Wind Beneath My Wings," Bette Midler version of course.

Blake and her dad danced too, and he made an appropriate toast thanking everyone for coming. Cary McCord was best man and recapped Blake and Scott's long relationship with many laughs and memories.

The dancing ensued. Scotty and Tom were on the dance floor. Scott had Tom on his shoulders as they danced wildly hands up in the air. Then suddenly Tom began to fall backwards. The room went silent. "I'm okay," he said as he grabbed Scott's hand to help him up. And the dancing resumed, and everyone was thankful our host was not injured.

The reception was over. The bride and groom had left the building. Louis was asleep on the sofa as I held Lindsay in my lap. Tom was in the office with the manager settling the bill when I noticed Blake's Mom carrying wedding gifts to her trunk with no help. I corralled some young guys, and we finished the job. She drove off by herself, as I wondered when Blake's Dad had disappeared.

Scott and Blake honeymooned in Vail Colorado on Marriott points Tom had collected. We knew the depth of their love and we were happy to be able to give them this sendoff.

My little boy was now a husband.

My brother Ernie and his growing family had moved to a small town just north of us, New Port Richey. Their military duties had taken them from Hawaii's Pearl Harbor, where they met, to a small California town. Ernie was happy to be daddy to his three girls and help the other military families during spouses' deployment with odd jobs that needed to be done. With their obligations both completed, they were able to finally move closer to family.

Brother had a love of carpentry and became an apprentice to a skilled California man who taught him masonry and other carpentry skills. Ernie soaked up all he could, increasing his talents.

Ernie and Yolanda had a deep faith that had saved them both from their worldly pasts. It was a miraculous transformation from the tough and reckless teenager I had known.

When we would talk, he would share his newfound faith. He was bringing up his girls in a much better environment then we had known.

It made me so thankful and proud to hear him speak about his love for Jesus and how his new belief system had truly saved him from a life of turmoil, sadness, drugs, and alcohol, a pattern he most certainly had now escaped.

God was sending me a strong example to follow through my younger brother and, I saw the beautiful fruits when they would visit. If He could change Ernie ... He could change anyone.

The way they spoke to one another, so calmly. How he expressed his love for his wife and children was clearly a gift from God. It was refreshing and made me proud of all he had overcome through faith.

Ernie started a business, Christian Builders, and told me how he would share the gospel with everyone he met.

Often Tommy and I would face a problem and say, "What would Ernie do?" like the popular phrase *WWJD*. *What would Jesus do?*

Tom continued to run the Palm Harbor office until Michael returned from his treatment cancer-free. It was now time for us to make the move to Jacksonville. Tom's trips north to call on Winn Dixie were frequent. The four-hour drive made it nearly impossible to drive back home same day. We couldn't escape the move any longer.

The bitter truth of the matter was I would have to relinquish my dream job as Training Director in the division office and I wasn't sure what the Sr. VP would say. Financially I needed to work.

Tom offered to give me my "dream house" for giving up my "dream job." We ordered a collection of house plans from Southern Living. In a few days, the *Hometown Collection* arrived with twenty floor plans to choose from.

When I got home that night Tom told me to look at the selection. He had already chosen the one he liked and now it was my turn. Not surprisingly ... we chose the exact same house, a Stephen Fuller design that reminded us both of our Mid-Western roots. It was a country house with porches wrapped around the front with white columns and shutters on the windows. It was perfect for our family. The house was a huge step up from our modest ranch house in Palm Harbor.

We had spent quite a bit of time in Jacksonville on weekends looking at different communities to decide where we wanted to live. The Sawgrass Marriott was our home when I would drive up with the kids on Friday night to spend time looking at houses and basking in the sun and surf of the beautiful Cabana Club right on a private stretch of beach on the Atlantic Ocean.

We agreed we loved the beach lifestyle and found a large lot that backed up to golf's TPC Sawgrass. After some negotiation we had made our decision and had even found a custom builder who was excited about our floor plan. We signed the deal with the builder. We were officially moving.

Having to drop this bombshell on my boss was difficult. We had worked together for most of my career and our relationship was much more than employee–boss. We were great friends.

While I had mentioned a potential move for our family for a couple of years, it always seemed somewhere in the distant future. Now the time had arrived. He took the news remarkably well and even arranged a position for me in the Jacksonville market without reducing my pay or benefits. There was nothing stopping us from the move. I was excited for this new chapter in our lives to begin

Maybe I didn't see it at the time, but I was letting go of the strongest personal lifeline I had. For most of my adult life, my career had defined me. I worked hard at it because I knew I had to. Now I was slowly letting go of this line and reaching for another one … my sweet Tommy. There was such an unfamiliar feeling of security in all of this. And it felt really, really, good.

With Dad gone, his wife decided to move back to Michigan with her friends. This left the condo available to Scott and Blake. They moved in and started their life together. It was a perfect situation for everyone. God was tightening all the loose ends.

Our house sold, we packed everything up to be placed in storage until our new house was finished. We were officially on to the next chapter of our lives.

38

The Move

WE RENTED A FURNISHED CONDO just a short bike ride from our lot. A day care center just outside our gated community made it easy to pick up the little ones now in first and second grade. They would be picked up from school in a van and taken one mile to after school care. It was safe and convenient.

Everything we needed was within a few miles from our home. Bank, school, church and a shopping center with supermarket and several small stores and restaurants located just outside our gate.

It was a typical tourist beach town. But the big draw was TPC Sawgrass and The PLAYERS Championship. The home of the PGA Tour administrative offices where the Commissioner of Golf for the entire PGA Tour were housed on the grounds of the country club. This is the pros headquarters, and many lived in nearby communities.

It wasn't long before Tommy met a friendly guy building on the next cleared lot to ours.

Quick introductions out of the way, Tommy asked, "What do you do?"

"I'm a pro golfer," said Fred Funk.

"Oh really?" Tom replied. "What do you hit?'

"Founders," he replied.

"Oh," Tom answered sounding disappointed.

Each day they would meet up on their bikes to access their slabs, meet with their builders and contractors, and discuss the project for the day. It was the beginning of a long friendship.

The homes and the game that would bring them together would reap so much fruit they could never have imagined.

My job, while a step back in responsibility, was challenging because of the situation I had placed myself in. My boss had decided the manager of this territory who had been in the position for several years was not performing. He was let go to the complete surprise of his loyal staff, not to mention his accounts.

Enter me! It appeared, and highly likely I might add, that a position had been created to accommodate my move to North Florida.

Within one month, silence smacked me in the face each morning as I walked into the office. I wasn't going to have it. After all, I was known to be one of the company's biggest cheerleaders. Positivity was my middle name. We were supposed to be having fun.

The staff just didn't trust me. After all, I had been responsible for their former bosses firing ... even if indirectly. I was forced to draw a line in the sand. Everyone had to decide if they were with me or against me.

Only one employee left, the person had been the source of discord for the entire office. The staff wanted a fresh start and new ideas for attaining the numbers that had for many, months not achieved. They saw I had that.

This was one of the most challenging times I had ever faced in my career. I was truly torn between feeling a strong obligation to jump into this pile of crap and fix it or running to pick up the kids from daycare and rush them to the beach to play in the golden hour tide pools.

Having worked my entire life, I couldn't wrap my brain around the possibility of not working. The mortgage on the new house, predicated on both our incomes, was signed. We were under construction and contracted to our builder. There was no turning back now from the house.

And, oh what a house it was! It was double the square footage of our last house. Every day Tom was adding more detail translating into change orders and change orders meant more cost. Wood trim around the windows, beefed-up crown molding and raising ceilings were justified in our minds by the fact we lived in a gated community directly across from the clubhouse and offices of the PGA Tour, not to mention a view of holes 3 and 4 of the famed Stadium Course. Our custom builder was as excited as we were to see the finished product.

The biggest draw in North Florida annually is The PLAYERS Championship. In 1982, TPC Sawgrass became their permanent home. To say Tom's family loved the sport would be a huge understatement. He dreamed of big parties the entire week of TPC. He knew his family would fly down from Ohio to fill our bedrooms just to attend this self-dubbed *fifth major* of the golf world.

The house was magnificent. It was our exaggerated version of the house with the white picket fence. We couldn't wait for the day the Certificate of Occupancy was signed and we would arrange for the moving company to deliver our furnishings. I could smell the garlic wafting through the house from my first pot of homemade spaghetti sauce. It wouldn't be home until that happened.

On April 15th, 1994, we wrote the final checks and were handed the keys officially and spent the night in the house we would call home for what we hoped was the rest of our lives.

Success was bittersweet that day as we also wrote a huge check to the IRS. It made us both a little nervous, and we awoke the first morning spooning as we looked out the un-curtained window overlooking the cart path and the first hole of the Dye Valley Golf Course wondering what had we done? And, secretly wondering how can we hold on to this gem?

A small black and white cat had been hanging out around the house for several weeks. The kids had fed the cat some milk thinking it was someone's lost pet. We later learned of a family of feral cats roaming the area. We agreed to let them keep the cat so long as it stayed outdoors. They would sit for hours on the porch stroking its back as "Oreo" purred a sweet thank-you for taking her in. She loved her new home as much as we did.

The plan for our children's education was set in stone. Tommy had grown up in Cleveland where there was a Catholic church or school on almost every corner. He credited his upbringing to the nuns who taught him, and he wanted the same for his children. Problem was the closest Catholic school had a three-year waitlist. We were forced to send them to the public elementary school with a great reputation just a ten-minute bus ride from home.

Our church home was established, and we hoped one day the kids would be able to attend Catholic school, but we had met a new family on the street. They were such fun, and the dad was principal at the public school they were attending. He assured us it was a good choice.

In fact, the family of four moved into their home that hot 4th of July weekend just a few houses down the street. We shared our mutual builder who was eager for us to meet. Tommy helped them move from the condo they had rented just outside the gate. They told us the air-conditioning was not working, so we offered to have them stay at our house. This was the beginning of a long and deep friendship, and after all, he was our children's principal.

The kids found that quite amusing.

The big yellow school bus stopped twice daily in front of our house. We installed a portable basketball hoop near our garage, and Tommy encouraged the kids to show up early for a game of hoops. It was a great time to meet the families moving in on the street. The parents would walk up with their coffee cups steaming and family dog on a leash to introduce themselves. We forged many long-lasting friendships right in our driveway.

It was clearly a new chapter in our lives, and we were excited about the possibilities.

39

We Will Go on the Quarterly Plan...

FIVE MONTHS AFTER WE MOVED in, I called Tom on the phone in tears.

"I just can't take it any longer."

Work had become unbearable. I had always been proud of the fact that I embraced change in our organization. In fact, I thrived on it. It was the best part of my job because it made me stretch and grow. But this time, management was implementing changes that would adversely affect business projections. After all, I had worked for over eighteen years in this market, and I attempted everything I knew of to increase the numbers. What they were proposing had failed before. There was no way it could work now.

The staff had come around. We were producing better numbers and they were feeling success winning incentive contests and higher pay increases than ever. These changes would take us back to square one.

Tom and I agreed I should arrange to fly to the home office and voice my opinion armed with statistics and hard proof that the plan they had implemented would not work as well as my own plan for success. If I had to take a strong line, he had told me to do what I needed to do.

As I sat across from the president of our company, not my SVP and friend, I felt confident. Why would they go to the expense of having me fly out if they didn't want to hear my thoughts?

Formalities out of the way, we dove into discussion. Stating my case, I made it clear I didn't agree with the changes being made and my plan to improve the numbers. Immediately I knew there would be no concessions.

Within ten minutes I agreed to hand in my resignation. I was shuffled to Human Resources for my exit interview.

It had happened so quickly. My twenty-seven-year career was over. They paid me a generous severance package and I was on a flight back to Jacksonville in a complete fog.

Before I boarded the plane, I called Tom to give him the bad news. I was thankful and will never forget this response.

"Come home to me and the kids. I never wanted you to work anyway."

He could not have said anything more perfect that night. I couldn't wait to get home to his loving arms and the faces of my smiling children.

The next morning as I collected my personal belongings from my office and said my farewells to the staff, my mind was filled with a million questions.

I had not expected the conversation to end in this way. I kept thinking in my mind, they were paying me three times the paygrade for the job. It was totally a business decision and not personal. At least that was what I hoped.

We sat at the kitchen table and discussed financially what it meant that I had no job. Tom's salary was commission-based. He was building his pipeline and things were going quite well. Could he sustain the expenses on his own? It was a huge undertaking.

Tommy and the kids were excited!

We agreed we would go on the quarterly plan. We would consider each quarter what we needed to do, and hopefully it wouldn't mean selling the house. Even though we were prepared to do what we needed to do.

It was as if God was orchestrating the entire thing, moving us, building a home, allowing me to be a stay-at-home mother to the children by quitting my job, giving my husband the financial resources to keep it all going, transitioning our family into what He had instructed in the Bible.

Our life was heading in the right direction even more clearly. It was truly unbelievable.

40

Reborn

W ALKING THE NEIGHBORHOOD DAILY BECAME my therapy. It felt good to spend my energy this way rather than trying to define my new self-worth. I didn't really know what I wanted to do with my life, but I contemplated many options on these daily hour-long walks.

I found solace in walking the sandy beach while the kids were at school examining my life in detail. I began to think about God and how He perceived me and what He might think about my leaving the job so abruptly. Did He view it as selfish? Was I too weak? Questions swirled through my mind like the tide pools beneath my bare feet.

It was a tumultuous time for me. I threw myself into my family. If not at a job, I would do everything for my husband and children to make their lives the best they could be right at home. I would show them the love I had for them by cooking a daily meal, ironing Tommy's shirts, cleaning the house and helping the kids with their schoolwork. I would volunteer at the school and walk faithfully every day. I prayed as I walked that God would show me what I was supposed to do.

A few months later the neighbor across the street invited me to attend a fashion show as her guest at one of the local private clubs. I agreed to go. She was a beautiful girl from Atlanta with a cute blonde flip and a thick Southern accent. Her family was wonderful, and our children had become friends.

The day of the fashion show I was seated with another new neighbor I had met at the bus stop as Mindy went about her duties. Carolyn and I shared stories about our kids and how they were adjusting to new schools. She was a delight, and I was thankful to sit with her in this large crowd of strangers.

As soon as the speaker at the head table began, I realized I had been invited to some sort of religious event. They blessed the food and we introduced ourselves at our table as we ate fresh salads and a nice lunch.

Beautiful models, members of the group, walked past us in cute resort wear from local boutiques. It was lovely. After the fashion show we were asked to get comfortable as they introduced the author of the book *Struck by Lightning, Then by Love* – Wilma Stanchfield.

Wilma was an engaging speaker and shared her miraculous story of how she and her husband while on a camping trip with their sons on a remote lake were struck by lightning and the awesome power of her agonizing ten-year search for peace and then her transformation once struck by God's love.

The story was captivating. The room was silent and many of us held back tears as she bared her soul to us.

Then she asked a question...

She asked if anyone else in the room had struggled with doubt, fear or pressure of time, and family, marital tension, business failure. It felt as if she was speaking directly to me. She continued to press forward and grab my heart right in the palm of her hand. She asked us to say a little prayer to ask Jesus Christ into my life, to take the controls of my life and to be my personal savior, to draw a line in the sand and give myself completely over to Him.

I said willingly and without equivocation. "I do." And the tears began to roll down my cheeks uncontrollably.

The luncheon was over, and I sat dazed in my chair unable to stand. I looked around the table certain I would see others with smeared makeup and stunned as I was. But no … I was the only one. I stood and moved slowly to the exit. A line had formed near the speaker, and I stood patiently until we were standing face to face.

Introducing myself I gave her a hearty hug. This woman was an angel and I had experienced something, I wasn't sure what, but it was deeply spiritual.

That day marked a turning point in life. Had I always felt I was religious? Absolutely! And, to my credit, I did all the things I felt a religious person should do. I attended mass, raised my children to be good Catholics, taught them their prayers, prayed before bedtime and before holiday meals. Everything … or so I thought.

Well, everything but the one most important part of all. I never really understood the love God had for me or shared the intimate relationship I later found He wanted with me my entire life. He wanted me to turn over the control of my life to Him completely.

As I got into my car to drive home and for the first time in several weeks, I felt light and clearheaded. And a peace I had never in my life felt washed over me.

That day I was truly born again, and nothing would ever be the same.

41

Soaking It All In

T HE NEXT DAY I RECEIVED a phone call from one of the ladies who had been sitting at the head table at the fashion show. She introduced herself and said she would like to get to know me. She said they were having a coffee the next week and invited me to attend. I agreed but silently I wondered if I had come upon a cult of some sort. They certainly were persistent. This was all new to me and honestly, I felt a bit manipulated.

God cleared my already empty calendar. When I arrived at the address I was greeted with loving arms. We sat in a circle as one of the older ladies opened in prayer.

She prayed a scripture I recognized Matthew 2:18 *Wherever two or three are gathered in my name, there am I in the midst of them.*

We sat just talking really. Each of the ladies shared about someone who was sick, someone who lost their job or was considering an abortion, someone who suffered the loss of a husband. They called these stories "prayer requests." There seemed much more serious than anything I felt I needed to pray for. (Our kids, family issues and transitioning from an all-consuming career.)

Once the last request had been made, some of the ladies began to pray specifically for each request made. But they were like no prayers I had ever heard before, not the *Hail Mary* or the *Glory Be* or the *Lord's Prayer*. They were almost like conversations, like God was sitting right here with us, and they were talking directly to Him. It was simply beautiful. And I again felt surrounded by that peace I had felt the week before.

As I went to leave, one of the ladies came up to ask me if I had ever done a Bible study. Practicing Catholicism, the answer was "No." I wasn't sure my church would even allow such a thing. We had studied the Catechism but not the Bible. I had a dust-covered Catholic family Bible someone had given me for a wedding gift. Which wedding was that?

Out of curiosity I agreed to attend. The next week I found myself at a table with a small book in front of me. This group was smaller, maybe six women. One was the leader and explained everything and some rules. Those who didn't have one were given a New Testament Bible. We began week one of a *Stonecroft Ministries*, non-denominational Christian, Bible study series "*Prayer.*"

A bit embarrassed I shared how my mother had taught me not to ask God for anything in prayer that wasn't important. I admitted she had told me He was busy answering everybody's prayers, so I shouldn't bother him with my trivialities. I didn't know how to pray except the rote prayers I had been taught. The group put me at ease telling me it was "all good" and that was what this study was all about. Again, I felt comfortable, unjudged, and at ease. I was beginning to love these ladies … every one of them.

For the next eighteen years, I attended or held Bible studies at my home with this new and ever-growing group of ladies collectively searching for answers to lifelong questions. They each shared life experiences and how important God was in their lives. We developed deep bonds that would carry all of us through the highest peaks and the lowest valleys life cast us.

This new part of my life was no mistake. I had always loved to entertain. I would search through my collection of cookbooks, trying to find the perfect thing to serve that was delicious, appealing, and creative. It was a chance to exercise my culinary skills and meet new people in the community. While I hadn't recognized it yet ... this group of friends had not happened accidentally.

God certainly knew how to hook me in.

During that time, my knowledge of Christ grew tremendously. My spiritual walk deepened. I wanted Christ not only in my life.... I wanted Him in the lives of my husband and children, even my friends. And I worked on this tirelessly.

Life had thrown Tommy and me many peaks and valleys over those years. But I felt prepared to handle just about anything with my newfound friend Jesus.

I felt His presence in my life grow closer and closer. Suddenly I realized all He had done in my past that had prepared me for the things that were happening today. The things He had planned for me. But I had never understood the plan began when I was fearfully and wonderfully made in the womb of my mother. I began to grasp the idea that His plan continues to this very day and even beyond.

42

Old and New Friends

Tom's three sisters came for a visit one spring about three years after we moved into our new home. They would enjoy the sun and the pool as we sipped on margaritas and laughed, telling stories of old times.

The pool phone rang and one of Tom's sisters, Mary, answered.

"Yes, this is Tommy's house." I heard her say.

"You are kidding me." Realizing this was one of Tommy's childhood friends, she listened as the guy on the other end explained he had been transferred to Florida.

"Where in Florida, Pat?" she asked.

"Well actually a beach town called Ponte Vedra," he answered.

"Gee," Mary said, that's where Tommy lives.

Pat explained he and his wife had just purchased a house in a gated community. He had been transferred by his company. It was on Seven Mile Drive.

Hardly able to believe it, Mary informed him that is where Tommy lives … Seven Mile Drive.

For the next month or so Pat would play golf with Tom, eat dinner, and tell us about his wife, daughter, and son who would be joining him as soon as they closed on the house.

Pat and Tom were born just two days apart. Both sets of parents belonged to the same parish, so they knew each other. The boys were delivered at St. Johns' Hospital and lay in the same nursery.

They would later attend school together, and as they grew; they would hang with the same group of friends. They lost track of each other when both left for college and then jobs.

Pat and Tommy picked up right where they had left off. And, when Pat's family arrived, we felt as if we had family right on our street. A deep friendship that exists even today would begin to blossom.

When I shared with Michele my experience with the Bible Study group, she appeared cautiously curious. I shared with her the newfound peace I had been feeling and asked her to join me at the next luncheon. She agreed.

Michele's testimony is beautiful and powerful. Our faith walk grew as we exercised and walked, daily sharing deep secrets as we learned to pray and see what God had been doing when neither one of us realized He was even present in our lives.

We grew to truly be sisters in Christ.

Our group of sisters was growing to be much more than neighbors and friends and Bible study sisters. They were more like family.

This move had resulted in us meeting and making lifelong friendships that would prove to be invaluable over the years as our lives unfolded and our children grew. Helping one another through the tough times with tears and prayers. Celebrating the good times with happy tears and laughs and continued prayers of thankfulness and gratitude for the blessing that He placed us together on this path through life.

43

The Players—Funk's Punks

THE PARTIES WE LOVED TO hold mainly around The PLAYERS Championship began in 1994.

Our friendship with Fred and Sharon Funk strengthened when we moved into our homes. Fred loved to swim after golf practice when he wasn't on tour, but he had no pool. One day while sitting around our pool just weeks before the PLAYERS, Tommy mentioned it would be fun to gather our new neighbors to follow Fred during the tournament. It seemed even better than following the crowded galleries of big-name pros. We needed T-shirts; we agreed. And a name for our group. "How about "Funk's ... something," Fred said with a grin on his face. Sharon immediately said, "*Funk's Punks*" and laughing, it was done. Arnie had his Army ... Funk has his Punks. Powder blue T-shirts arrived a week later, and we were officially Fred Funk's fan club.

We even joined Fred on tour. During the Florida swing, he played at Bay Hill in the Arnold Palmer Invitational. We packed up the kids, the guys grabbed their clubs, and off we went to Orlando. The moms took the kids to Disney parks during the day while the dads played golf or followed Fred. It was a great time. And Fred seemed to delight in the antics the boys would pull after many celebratory beers/shots for each birdie Fred would make. It got a bit rowdy. But when Tommy asked if they should settle down Freddy yelled "make it louder." And they didn't disappoint.

The next year Fred scored another great endorsement, Cutter Buck. They provided a discount for our logoed golf shirts. Now the "Punks" had a uniform. The shirts were a bright orange "tangelo" which we paired with navy shorts. We even had shirts for the girls and logoed navy-blue golf hats for everyone. People could notice us walking the course behind our leader, a sea of bright orange shirts.

You could hear them whisper then laugh. "Here comes Freddy and his Funk's Punks."

The parties grew bigger as the fan club membership increased. One afternoon I remember Lindsay running up the sidewalk from the school bus embarrassed to tears. "Momma why do we have a circus tent in our back yard?" She was referring to the thirty-foot tent, tables, and chairs to protect Funk's Punks from the elements and provide a comfortable place to sit.

One of the neighbors owned a digital graphics company that produced fabric signs for businesses. We asked Sharon for some photos of Fred and suddenly we had several larger-than-life-size banners we hung from the trees, the sides of the tent, and one huge face of Fred from our rooftop. The Goodyear Blimp captured that one.

It was interesting to hear the comments from the gallery on four-tee box of the TPC Stadium course that overlooks our house. Most fans remarked, "That must be Fred Funk's house," said a fan.

"I know, he lives here," said another.

Fred always said, "Like I would hang huge pictures of myself on my house." But it was all great fun.

The parties began the weekend before the tournament when Tom's parents, aunt, and uncle would arrive. The spare bedroom was designated for Lugi and Peggy and Lindsay would give hers to Aunt Maryann and Uncle Jug. Each bedroom had a private bathroom, so it was comfortable for all. Lindsay slept in Louis' bunk beds for the week. Uncle Jug always made it appealing by leaving them a crisp Benjamin in an envelope on their dressers the last day of their trip.

Tommy had planned every meal from beginning of the week to the end of the next. His folks love a good meal and don't like to eat in. We had reservations at the best places around town. While eating breakfast, we would undoubtedly be discussing where we would have lunch and dinner for the day. No reservation? You were probably out of luck in this town PLAYERS week.

The practice rounds began on Monday morning. Our visitors would carry their golf chairs to hole 3 where they would camp out for the day. They watched silently as the pros made their way through just a few feet beyond the entrance gate steps from our backyard. It was the week they looked forward to each year.

Tuesday the tents, tables, and chairs went up in our yard. Soda fountain and beer kegs arrived on Thursday and often a barrel-tapping party ensued.

Friday was family day. Everyone who had bought a ticket was welcome. The caterers made hot dogs and tuna sandwiches for lunch, along with banana pudding and coleslaw. Friday night was chicken dinner with cornbread and all the fix-ins.

The same caterers had worked our party since the beginning, and they never let us down. The smell of burning wood filled the air as food was prepared on site on a huge black barrel BBQ pulled on a trailer behind the box truck that read *Country Caterer's—We specialize in Whole Hogs.* They knew where every electrical plug, water source, or light switch was located. So, Tommy and I could literally leave them in charge of the house visit the tournament and as we walked home over the hill, overlooking our house at the end of the round the caterers would be serving hors d'oeuvres. We would freshen up and join the merrymaking.

We charged the neighbors $100 per head for the entire week of festivities. They only needed to purchase their tickets to the tournament for a week's worth of unbelievable entertainment. It became the most coveted ticket in town.

Friday night's we hired a DJ. The kids especially enjoyed dancing around the pool deck as the parents adoringly looked on. Fred would appear after finishing his round and cleaning up. Once he arrived, we chain danced around the pool to *"Play that Funky Music"*, Fred, our leader at the head of the chain. Once the children left, drinks would flow, and the dancing continued into the night.

We had one close friend who led the ladies to a group dance. Michael was a true life of the party kind of guy. He would stand on one side of the pool, hands on his hips, and point to the cast of girls across the water waving instruction for their next choreographed move. It was provocative and fun, and we all looked forward to his finale fav *"Sweet Caroline"* once his back gave out. "Bah, Bah Bah…"

The police visited a couple of times each year to remind us at 10 PM we had to shut it down due to the local noise ordinance. And we would promptly obey.

Later, the group dubbed *Circle of Trust*, would form ritually around the fireplaces into the early morning hours contemplating life and enjoying the company and fresh air.

On Saturday night, we offered a sit-down dinner under the softly lighted tents and more formal linens, real plates, and silver. The dinner of steak and baked potato with salad and a dessert we considered "adult night—no children allowed."

We hired a real band and again we partied with Fred. Over the years, pros and caddies showed up at the party. One year, Peter Jacobsen grabbed a guitar from the band and joined in, to everyone's delight, for a surprise set.

After seven days of partying, Sunday was a quiet day. The tents were left up. But the bartenders and the caterers were gone. Our group would sit on the grass of notorious hole number 17, The Island Green, watching the final round and betting on the players closest to the pin as we watched the winners round the final turn.

And then it happened ... our leader Fred Funk became the oldest player at forty-eight to win the 2005 PLAYERS Championship in a rain-delayed Monday final round between Luke Donald, Tom Lehman, and Scott Verplank, in blustery conditions.

Course rangers had been warned the Funk's Punks might jump into the chilly water on 18th green should Fred win the PLAYERS. We were surrounded as we jumped to our feet when he sunk the final putt to the crowds' cheers. The Funk's Punks beyond thrilled never neared the water.

God was surely shining down between the fog and the raindrops that day.

44

Twins

LOUIS AND LINDSAY WERE THRIVING in this small beach town. They loved the ocean and had plenty of friends and doing good in the public school we had fought so desperately to avoid.

When he stepped off the school bus each day, Louis would exchange his backpack for his golf bag and off he would march to the practice range. He had a budding love for the game.

He really had no clue how privileged he was having access to TPC Sawgrass. When Fred was in town, he would grab Louis in his golf cart as he headed over to the private area where the pros practiced. It was not unusual for Louis to practice next to local pros Vijay Singh, David Duval, or Rocco Mediate. One day David Duval asked Louis what shoe size he wore and tossed him a pair of worn golf shoes.

Lindsay had a core group of girlfriends. Rather a tomboy, she enjoyed climbing trees or jumping waves in the sea with friends at a nearby beach club. She was a spunky tween in search of her own style. She loved to karaoke in her room microphone in hand, arms reaching to the sky as she belted out her favorite Disney song. Often, she and her friends jumped on the bed singing their hearts out.

Lindsay ran our house and we learned early we needed to keep a short leash on her for her own protection. We laughed … she was completely in control of us.

This led to Friday night pizza and a movie at the "Z House." We would encourage both to invite their friends as we loaded up the Ford Explorer and headed to the beach theatre for an appropriate movie. After the show, we noshed on pizza before heading back to the house. It became a weekly happening we all looked forward to.

Tommy was the greatest Dad. He loved being surrounded by kids. Our house was designed with that in mind, so there was a designated room over the garage complete with a large-screen TV, video games, karaoke, and even *Skeeball*. They could gather, do what they wanted. And we could pop in easily just to check. The noise wouldn't bother anyone.

Scott and Blake were growing their little family in Palm Harbor just three hours away. Christmas Eve, two years after they married, they presented us with our first grandchild … a beautiful little pink bundle named Taylor. We couldn't have been happier. My baby boy had given us a baby. The love we felt for her and the future grandchildren was huge and it only grew right along with them.

They got along great and worked hard to provide a good life for their little family. Scott was in sales and Blake was a primary school teacher. They were known affectionately in their small Gulf side town as "Mr. and Mrs. Palm Harbor" active in sports, school, and church. We didn't have to worry about either of them.

Just fourteen months later along came our little Abby. Blake decided to take a break from teaching to care for the little ones, and Scott was more than happy.

My Mom was happy with husband number three in her paid-for condo decorated in bright colors. (She had been diagnosed with macular degeneration, and one of the indicators was surrounding yourself with brilliant colors.) They could be found under the tiki-hut enjoying an afternoon cocktail most days.

About once every few months I would take a trip to visit but would stay with Blake and Scott. I never felt comfortable staying in the condo with Mom and Number Three. He was nice enough, but they would start drinking at noon and wouldn't stop till they were snoozing early evening. They only visited my home once when her sister Aunt Lil and brother, Uncle Dick, and wife Aunt Jackie had come down from Michigan. We took them out for dinner. They left early in the morning.

Two years later, while life was sailing along beautifully. I took a call from Scott. He sounded upset and I knew Blake had recently found out she was pregnant once again. They were not sure they could afford another baby and with Blake not working they were beginning to feel the strain on their finances. I worried there was something wrong because they were scheduled for a doctors' appointment that day.

"Mom, I have something to tell you, "He struggled to say.

"Scott, what is it?" I responded.

"Is Blake okay? Is everything okay?"

"Mom, we are having TWINS," he announced in a voice filled with trepidation. "I don't know what I am going to do. We can barely afford one more baby, let alone two. And there is no way Blake would be able to go back to work."

"There is never a time in your life when you feel you can afford your children. God wouldn't do this to you if it wasn't meant to happen," I added confidently.

He settled down instantly. Those calming words, letting him know that God was in control, not him, seemed to make all the difference that day. And frankly, those words were a source of comfort for all of us on many other occasions as well.

God was blessing us in a huge way with two more little angels. We embraced the idea. And I assured him it was going to be fine. He had a family that would see to it that all went smoothly.

45

Bible Thumper?

T OM'S BUSINESS WAS DOING WELL. He had made significant improvement in the local account he was responsible for. And his partners were excited about it too.

The three partners, while devoted friends, had distinct styles of how to run the business. D and Z worked out an agreement and bought out the originator, C of CDZ Sales. It was a complex buy out, but the attorney brought them all to agreement.

Signed, sealed, and delivered Tommy now owned fifty percent of the business. He and his partner D could focus on the changes they had agreed would take the business to the next level.

Tom imagined a warehouse in Jacksonville. A 25,000-square-foot space where they could set up shelving like a grocery store filling the shelves matching the planograms specific to each product line they represented. Manufacturers could arrange a time slot with their respective buyers, fly in to handle seasonal buying appointments all in one day. It made sense to the buyer and vendors he ran it by. A completely unique concept to the industry and everyone endorsed it.

They found space, purchased shelving, and set up the warehouse just as imagined. The staff would prepare bid sheets and P.O.s to handle all orders. He offered breakfast and lunch to everyone, a welcome surprise. The concept streamlined the process for everyone. It worked and the business thrived.

Louis worked as the Warehouse Manager while he was in high school and college, cleaning and stocking the shelves and managing the deliveries of new products that arrived daily ready to be presented to the buyers. It was good experience for him. The work was physical, and he had the opportunity to be present when the seasonal shows took place, meeting the top-level management of companies they represented as well as the buyers from corporate grocery/retail headquarters throughout the southeast. His Dad would ask him to be a fourth in golf on many occasions, allowing him to meet many of the customers. He was learning the business from the ground up and forming relationships that would eventually open many doors for him.

My faith life was thriving. I had replaced the career that had provided me what I needed with a new set of survival skills. I was like a sponge absorbing everything I could about God and how to change my life to make it pleasing to Him.

The Bible study groups grew in number. I invited my friends to attend too. I couldn't wait to see the reaction of my close friends to this new life that brought a sense of peace and strength I had never felt before. I wanted everyone to know my Heavenly Father the way I was getting to know Him. I was bold and I didn't care if they called me a "Bible thumper." I wanted everyone to feel the peace I now had.

On mornings when the ladies would come for prayer coffee, before Tom had the warehouse, he would sneak along the second-floor loft to the bathroom in the spare bedroom. The floor creaked and his cover was blown. We all found it very amusing.

He didn't know how to react at first to my newfound faith. He had been the one who made sure we make it to mass on Sunday and gathered the family around for the dinner prayer.

His faith was a very private side of him. He didn't find it necessary to share with others outside the family what he believed or if he prayed or read the Bible. He had attended all-boy Catholic schools and had a good theological background. He wasn't comfortable discussing his beliefs with strangers or even with his friends.

I am sure he thought I had taken this whole religion thing too far when I asked him to reconsider some of the places he visited with his friends after football games.

Had I turned into a holy roller?

46

A "Funky" World

I T WAS SUMMER 2005, A few months after Fred Funk had won The Players Championship. To his surprise he was invited to play the LG Skins Game in LaQuinta, CA. Another surprise for Fred and all of us was his outstanding win of $925,000 and 15 skins, a record for a rookie.

As the oldest player at forty-nine to play in a skins game, Tiger Woods told Fred he would never live it down if Annika Sorenstam outdrove him on even one hole. Well, it did happen and Fred good naturedly pulled a pink skirt out of his bag and pulled it over his pants to finish the hole. The crowd loved it and so did the media.

During the presentation of the check, Fred looked straight into the camera and said, "JT, this is for you."

A few weeks before some friends of Fred and Sharon had introduced them to a young Episcopal School senior who had taken a hit that previous fall on the football field and suffered a near fatal spinal cord injury, leaving him in a wheelchair and unable to move from the neck down. Fred visited JT to inspire and encourage the young man whose life had been tragically changed instantly. However, during the meeting Fred himself felt inspired and lifted-up. He was amazed at the young man's attitude and positivity, brought on by his deep faith in God.

JT was the oldest of three children born to Jerry and Carmen Townsend. His two younger sisters idolized JT and he loved his family. His mother had taught all three of her children to trust in God at an early age. And, when this incident occurred, she drew on that faith to bring all of them to be able to face the challenges that lay before them.

The battery-powered wheelchair that allowed JT to be as mobile as possible was too large to fit into the family bungalow. They were forced to split up. JT lived in his Aunt Pat's home that had been made wheelchair accessible.

Fred called Tommy and me one afternoon and said he had someone he wanted us to meet. He told us the story of JT Townsend and we arranged to visit Aunt Pat's home to meet his family on a Sunday after church. Fred said he had an idea that he needed our help with.

We picked up some pastries and headed toward the address in downtown Jacksonville. When we pulled into the driveway of the small yellow house with a wheelchair ramp out front, we could never have guessed how this meeting would change not only our lives but the lives of our children and grandchildren forever.

We were welcomed by Aunt Pat and entered the small living room where chairs and sofas had been pushed against the wall to make room for JT's wheelchair. We were introduced to the Townsend family as well as Uncle Bobby, JT's parents Jerry and Carmen, his sisters Precious and Sunshine and many cousins. They were all so loving.

The guys talked sports and got to know one another. The ladies talked about JT's incident and reported on his many surgeries and physical therapy. JT had been cared for at Shepherd Center in Atlanta and they were encouraged by his progress. They also shared beautiful stories of the many nurses and doctors and the ESJ parents and families who had banded together to help them in a million ways.

The most amazing thing about that visit that day was the smile on JT's face and the twinkle in his eyes. You could never imagine how a young man headed to college on a football scholarship could handle the trial he was given. Yet he did with grace and faith in Jesus Christ.

Fred wanted to build the family a wheelchair accessible home so they could all be together, and JT would have the features he needed to live his best life.

Tommy and I cried most of the way home as we spoke to Fred and told him we were in for anything he asked us to do.

Fred and Sharon got busy. They found a beautiful double corner lot in a nice section of town, and with the Townsend's approval for the project they asked the PGA Tour to pay for the land. They agreed.

Tommy had introduced Fred to the owners of Cordelle Builders at our TPC party. Fred contacted them and they agreed to build the house. Their designer worked with JT's nurses to design the entire home to be accessible and safe for him. Including a lift over his bed that carried him into his open shower where a special chair was waiting.

Sharon contacted Pottery Barn, Williams Sonoma, and Viking who all agreed to help us furnish the home. My job was to fill the house with everything they needed. Fred told me he wanted them to move in with only their suitcases.

I went on radio and television asking the community to visit JT's registry with Bed Bath and Beyond and Target to purchase the household items they would need. Everyone had heard the story of this tragedy and wanted to help. I remember checking the registries to see what was happening and just as I would add more items, the word "complete" would pop up. It was truly a community act of love and kindness. We placed coin boxes at local restaurants and were amazed at the response from such a generous and loving community.

Fred and Sharon funded a special Trust, and a board was formed to oversee the expenses and the fund so the family could remain in the home for as long as they wished.

The week between Christmas and New Year that year, the Townsend family was told not to visit the house. The building was completed. Our smallest grandchildren helped clean windows while the rest of the girls in the family hung artwork, made beds with new linens and bedding, lined and organized cupboards and closets. One family, our dear friends Rich and Lynda even donated a complete dining room, furniture, a rug, crystal, dinnerware, and placed an FSU-decorated Christmas Tree in the corner. It was truly miraculous to see everyone excitedly pitching in to make our project just perfection.

The day of the house dedication Fred and Sharon and the Townsends had invited local pastors, the builders and contractors, the media, the Trust Board, ESJ students and parents and all who had been involved in making Fred's dream a reality. Making a beautiful accessible home where JT could be safe and comfortable.

Finally, JT and his family arrived, and the tears began to flow. The presentation of the house to this deserving family was one of the best days of our lives.

Fred and Sharon Funk had blessed the Townsend Family with a home they could all enjoy together safely and comfortably for many years to come. Their vision had made it all possible. Our involvement, just helping where we were needed, gave us all a sense of giving. It was an overwhelming feeling of sharing and caring I shall never forget. We were stewards following a divine plan that would improve the Townsends lives.

As a board member, I discovered approximately $25K annually would fall short of the budget. We decided to coordinate a fundraiser at a local sports bar during TPC week to raise money to pick up the shortage. T-shirts, hats, silent auction, donated food, beverages, beer and wine, a band called *Pro-Bono*, and volunteers lovingly pitched in. We sold tickets and everything combined we would make up the budget deficit each year. The Funk's Punks group grew, and the true spirit of the group just shined. Channel 12 who had been there from the date of the incident covered our party and shared the story of our community effort.

As time went on JT had a dream to repay the community that so generously helped him and his family when they needed help most. He and I agreed to form The JT Townsend Foundation with a mission of helping children and adults with disabilities with expensive adaptive equipment often denied by insurance as well as financial assistance.

Even the legal help we needed to draw up the 501c3 was donated by an ESJ dad who owned a law practice in town, Tommy Donahoo. He continues to handle our legal work to this day free of charge.

With the support of all the businesses and families like the Pappas family, Alberto and Valerie de la Torre, Karen and Don Wolfson, Dr. Julie Buckley, and so many more, we were able to make JT's dream come true.

His dream his foundation was such a blessing to the disabled community. JT delivered every piece of equipment personally with only one request ... pay it forward.

Here is a speech JT wrote and delivered to the Westside Rotary Club.

Hello, my name is JT Townsend.

The night of October 8, 2004, started like any other night for a typical high school football player. I attended Episcopal School of Jacksonville, and we were playing our main rival, Bishop Kenny High School, and were doing well. We had a great pre-game dinner, looked good during warm-ups, and took the field ready to win. Because the schools are only a mile apart, the stands were filled with students and parents. As one of the leaders of our defense, it was my job to rally our younger players and keep them in the game. I was the coach on the field, and although I was not the loudest or most hyper player, I led by example and hard work.

The tackle was just like hundreds of others I had made since I was ten years old: knees bent, head up, arms out. I don't remember the hit. I heard that I turned blue actually laying there in the grass. For me to turn blue—that had to be a bad sign.

The ambulance took me to Wolfson's Children's Hospital here in Jacksonville where my neck was stabilized, and I was given a halo—a circle of metal drilled into my skull that attached to my shoulders and immobilized my head. My C2 vertebra had been crushed in the accident, and I had no feeling below my neck. I then spent the next 4 months at UF Shand's trauma center with some of the best doctors in the region. The only problem, however, was that the doctors and nurses kept telling me all these things I would not be able to do—finish school, go to college, have a normal next 10 years. I knew then that I would have my doubters. I knew then I would prove them wrong. I knew then that I would overcome. I knew then that I would turn this setback into an opportunity.

I was fortunate to spend several weeks in rehab at the Shepard Center in Atlanta, a hospital that specializes in spinal cord injuries. Without the resources there I would not have been able to learn about the opportunities available to me such as my pacer that helped me breathe and my chair with the sip and blow straw to move around. Sure—I had my dark days. The days where I cried. The days where I wanted to join my friends and swim in the ocean. The days where I wanted to go shoot hoops in the driveway with my sisters. The days where I asked God why me? The amazing thing is that God answered. He wanted to use me as an instrument of healing and helping. I can do more from this chair than people think.

The community rallied behind me the whole way. Local high schools, especially Episcopal, kept my name front and center and made sure that I was not forgotten. The rest of the year went quickly—I was able to finish high school and enjoy my high school graduation with my family sitting on the front row.

I applied to and was admitted to UNF, where I enrolled in 2005. Obviously, I was not the traditional college student! My college career began with a thud – the car would not start on the day I was supposed to begin classes. I had other roadblocks, both real and symbolic, along the way. I had to re-learn how to study. I had to ask others for help. For someone who was shy and quiet, this was tough! At UNF, I learned about the power of teamwork, the power of community, and the power of joining together to support a common cause.

That's when I started having the dream for the Foundation. For several years, though, I had been turning dreams into realities, doing things that others told me I would never do. So many people in our community are worse off than me. I knew I had to start giving back more to support the community that that supported me when I needed it most. In Luke, Chapter 12, Jesus says, "To whom much is given, much is required." Because I had been given so much, I knew that God would require much of me.

About 3 years ago I started the JT Townsend Foundation, a non-profit group that awards grants to families with children who have severe developmental disabilities. This year, through God's help, we were able to distribute about $85,000 to 35 different families in Jacksonville. The foundation has a nice buzz going in the city. We are hooked into the Players Championship, the Jags, and other events in town. We look to grow and keep helping others wherever the need arises.

Only with God's grace can I keep going. Thank you and please look out for those who are less fortunate than you are.

Every day in life we are presented with choices. What we do with those choices determines who we are in life. I can't change what happened to me but with the right choices I can change the lives of others. We all have a purpose in life and true success comes when we realize our purpose. I think the two most important days in our lives are the day we were born and the day we realize why we were born. I now have a vision and a purpose and with the grace of God I have strength, courage, and determination.

Thank you and God bless you and all those less fortunate than us.

The JT Townsend Foundation continues on today, helping families with special needs living on Florida's First Coast, making their lives more family-inclusive and safer by donating pieces of adaptive equipment they could not otherwise afford.

47

Breaking News

June 2013

THE PHONE CALLS FLOWED IN consistently from board members, friends, and family as well as media, so many questions. While we were all aware of JT's physical condition and worked each day to provide all he needed to be comfortable, safe and productive, I never had taken my thoughts to the place we were today. I don't think any of us were prepared for his passing. We all were curious to know exactly what happened.

The doctors wanted to do an autopsy to determine the exact cause of death, but Carmen didn't want that. She wanted her son's body to remain intact. She believed he had been put through too much physically. Now, in this time, he should be at peace.

The doctors believed he died of an aneurysm, a blood clot that traveled to his heart or brain and took him instantly, with little or no pain. This was the only explanation they could give without an autopsy.

The media was asking us to provide final plans as soon as possible. We needed to get to work. Someone needed to spearhead this effort and we had the perfect person.

Scott Ross, the President of the Irrevocable Trust, and I had worked together since the formation of the team that Fred assembled to build the house. He would be the ones to plan next steps.

We set up the dining table with our laptops and phones and began the difficult conversations with JT's parents and family of the wishes they had for the next few days and weeks.

Visitors were restricted to family and a few friends and board members for this difficult day. Carmen refused to face the media yet. Media was very respectful of this request and continued to send their questions through me.

There was only one news anchor Carmen wanted to speak with, Jeannie Blaylock from First Coast News. Jeannie had followed JT's story from the beginning and did so with grace and love. When Jeannie called requesting an interview, I explained she would be the only one allowed this privilege.

There was an eerie silence in a house filled with people. The doorbell would ring as another platter of food arrived. Someone sent a beautiful wreath for the door adorned in garnet and gold ribbon, JT's favorite Florida State University colors, and bright sunflowers. His name "JT Townsend" glued in foil letters to the ribbon that crossed the center of the wreath. It was the perfect reminder that anyone who entered was entering a very sacred place.

Around three in the afternoon, my cell phone rang. It was Gus Bradley, head coach of the Jacksonville Jaguars. He wanted to get a message to JT's parents if possible.

I felt Carmen would want to take this call, knowing JT's love for the team. She agreed and I handed her my phone.

"Mrs. Townsend, this is Gus Bradley, I wanted to call and personally tell you how sorry we are to hear of JT's passing. JT held a very special place in the Jaguar organization. We loved having him visit our training camp. I always considered him a huge inspiration and motivation to our players. As you know, many of them considered JT a personal friend."

Carmen was visibly touched by the phone call as she shared with Coach just what the Jaguar team meant to her son.

"Well, I also wanted you to know that JT was going to be hired by the sales department in the fall. He was going to officially become a part of the organization himself," said Coach Bradley.

This was another dream that would have come true for this miraculous young man.

This was the first of many conversations she would encounter over the next few days that shed light on how her son had impacted others. We all had our stories and now was the time to share them.

The next two days we each received our tasks. There was much to be done. The funeral service at the church, a venue large enough to hold at least a thousand people, a program, phone calls to the honored guest list, all were important components of this celebration.

President of University of North Florida, and former Mayor of the City of Jacksonville, John Delaney, had been in contact with Scott Ross. It was high school graduation season, but he wanted to offer the use of the UNF arena for the celebration of life if we would consider it. It was perfect … JT's alma mater, large enough to hold six thousand three hundred people, centrally located, and good parking. Scott and a coordinator would work out date and time.

Surely God himself was involved in this plan.

JT and I had been on several segments of the local FCN show *First Coast Living* discussing the JT Townsend Foundation and upcoming fundraising events as well as sharing the good things we were doing for the disabled community living on the First Coast. The anchors, Nick Loren, Casey DeSantis, Curtis Dvorak, and more seemed to love having us on the show. Everyone was always touched by JT's spirit.

Nick Loren's face popped up on my phone. Nick is a local actor and Emmy-nominated talk show host who earlier in his career was known as stunt double for John Travolta. He was calling.

"Judi, I am so sorry to hear the news," he said. "I just can't believe it. Are you okay? Is everyone okay?" he asked.

We shared a moment.

The JT Townsend Foundation had coordinated a toy drop for the past several years at Nemours Children's Hospital. Nick played Santa and JT sat beside him as they surprised over three hundred sick young patients of Nemours Children's Hospital with Christmas presents. It was one of our favorite events of the year.

Nick saw the heart of JT those days and a friendship ignited.

"What can I do to help Judi?" Nick asked.

"I have an idea," I replied.

"I thought it would be great to have music at the celebration of life. What about that gospel choir you had on FCL recently?" I asked.

"Give me the details and let me get on it," Nick agreed energetically.

This was going to be the best celebration of life anyone had ever attended. We were going to love on JT's family and friends while honoring him in this perfect way.

Carmen and Jerry were holding up well along with Aunt Pat and JT's sisters Sunshine and Precious. The board had approved for the family to make final arrangements. Everything was moving along nicely until this happened...

The hospital called to advise Carmen they had removed JT's eyes and would be getting them to the next deserving applicant on the organ list.

Completely unaware of JT's decision, Carmen didn't see this as something extraordinary. She didn't want her baby's body to be desecrated in any way. JT's shining eyes were truly the gateway to his beautiful soul. She was very upset.

This called for a family discussion. Aunt Pat, Jerry, and Carmen's sisters rallied around her explaining this was a gift JT had requested himself. As an adult, he had the right to say he was an organ donor. And he had. It was typical JT.

She had no choice. She had to accept her son's wishes. But it didn't mean she was happy about it.

Finally, the day for the celebration arrived. The UNF arena greeted those who wished to view JT's body and pay their final respects. The service began with a beautiful hymn performed by the choir Nick had assemble, dubbed that morning to be forever known as the "JT Townsend Memorial Choir."

The arena was filled with a proverbial "who's who" of Jacksonville including a host of Jacksonville Jaguars and their wives, administrative staff including Coach Bradley and his wife Michaela, City of Jacksonville Mayor Alvin Brown, Episcopal School of Jacksonville Headmaster, Charlie Zimmer, parents, students and staff, fellow football and basketball teammates were among those seated. JT Townsend Foundation Board members and JTTF recipients were there in full force. Just about every pastor in the city would be on the stage to speak to the life of this young man.

Nick Loren led the memorial program. After some brief comments, Mayor Alvin Brown approached the podium. Within moments he was preaching from the pulpit.

"Today we celebrate the life of one of Jacksonville's own. JT Townsend was in all truth Jacksonville's son."

"We thank God for sending us this man who inspired us every day of his young life…"

I watched from my vantage point sitting on stage to the right of the city's most influential leader as he described the life of our beloved friend, his heels leaving the floor as he cried out "Hallelujah and thank you Jesus for sending us your son JT."

Each of the pastors had similar stories as they reflected on the spiritual life of this amazing young man. How his faith in his Lord and Savior Jesus Christ had given him the strength to face with unbelievable courage and fortitude the difficult journey he had traveled.

Then it was time for me to speak about my beautiful friend.

"We are humbled by the sentiments and the words that have been texted, posted, emailed, printed, tweeted, videoed and spoken about our dear sweet friend JT Townsend.

Words like perseverance, inner-strength, infectious smile, obedient and faithful servant, just a few.

Jacksonville Jaguar Coach Bradley said about JT…" He just drew you in the way he saw things … you just wanted to be around him…." And that is so true.

People want to be around positive people.

We all agree JT was all of those words and so much more. But all you have to do is look at his mother ... Carmen Townsend. All those things describe her as well. She raised that man to be all of that and more. While JT is our hero today ... so are Carmen and Jerry Townsend. These qualities we are speaking of do not happen organically. They must be cultivated.

This young man lived a life few of us could have lived with such grace."

Former Jacksonville Jaguar player Richard Collier said, "I understand how hard it is to keep smiling all the time, but JT never let you down." He kind of made me know that life goes on."

We all have choices. We can live a life that radiates the light of "peace and joy" or not.

This week you have read the stories about how JT would deliver the pieces of equipment to most of the 60 families JTTF was able to help. Inevitably, I would hear back from them how surprised they were that JT himself would take the time to come sit with them and just talk. The one common thread was always that he changed their outlook on the situation they had been dealt.

The First Coast community has been blessed to have seen firsthand his example.

Even after death, JT continued to "GIVE". JT had made the choice to be an organ donor for his eyes, his eyes that were perfect and loving and saw right into your soul. Those twinkling eyes are now providing JT's view of the world to some local person who was fortunate to receive them. JT

NEVER gave up and I know he is smiling down today from heaven and God is saying "Son, job well done."

We can bless HIM by living that example....

Let's all try to LIVE LIKE JT...

Imagine what the world would be if everyone LIVED LIKE JT."

I took my seat as Scott Ross concluded the tributes with a glowing eulogy and a military salute to the coffin.

Finally, the choir sang out with enthusiasm as we all sat in silence, soaking in the program and thanking God for sending us such a man as this.

My life, as well as that of countless others, was forever changed by my friendship with JT Townsend. JT showed me my purpose. He showed me how someone who was dealt a difficult hand could play it through with complete grace and gratitude. He used his situation to show complete faith in the God He loved.

Yes, my life would be forever changed. I knew what God wanted me to do. He wanted me to keep JT's legacy alive through the JT Townsend Foundation, helping children and adults living with disabilities and finding themselves in similar situation to JT with adaptive equipment that insurance denies and financial assistance to help when a single mother of a special needs child must miss work to sit next to their hospital bed. I knew what I needed to do.

I called an emergency board meeting of the JT Townsend Foundation.

The JT Townsend Foundation Board of Directors included several from the JT Townsend Irrevocable Trust Board. Each of the members brought with them a skill necessary to successfully run a business, plus they shared in our passion to carry out JT's wishes.

On the board we had seated a lawyer, an accountant, a marketing person, a web designer, physical therapist, and more. Each one of these members donated their time and expertise to the mission. And each one had a deep connection to JT himself. Most of them were parents of fellow classmates of JT. And, sadly, most of them had witnessed the "incident" on the football field October 4th, 2004. Their contribution was important to this grassroots non-profit. It enabled us to operate at an extremely low expense ratio, very important to donors today.

The vote was unanimous to keep JTTF running. We had seen the difference we had made in the sixty-some families we had already helped. We realized the need was so much greater than we had ever anticipated.

It was official. We would continue our good works, and I would continue as Executive Director and fundraiser. There was much work to be done.

Donations began to roll in from around the city as well as applications for assistance. We were still in business.

Summer rolled by as we tried to pick up the pieces of our broken hearts and push forward. The foundation was flourishing. People were eager to support us and volunteer to help. It was further confirmation what we were doing was God's work.

Casey DeSantis, the Channel 12 new anchor and host of *First Coast Living*, contacted me to ask a very serious question. She wondered if the Townsend family would allow her to write and produce a documentary on JT's life and legacy. I agreed the idea was spectacular.

"JT's story is one that needed to be shared." she said. And I could not have agreed more.

After talking with Carmen, JT's Mom, she agreed to allow Casey to interview the entire family and those touched by JT. Old home movie clips were turned over to Casey and she began her magic of writing the script and piecing together all she could get her hands on to document JT's amazing life.

When she was finished, she had produced a Suncoast Emmy-nominated documentary called, "*CHAMPION, the JT Townsend Story.*"

With the help of her co-host Nick Loren, we arranged a private screening of the film days before it was scheduled to air in a prime-time slot on Channel 12.

The headmaster of the Episcopal School offered their large auditorium for viewing and invitations were circulated to ESJ parents, teachers, and JTTF friends and recipients. Many of JT's coaches and those present the night of the incident were in the film and were excited to see the finished product. JT's large family sat in the front rows of the theatre as the movie was introduced by the beautiful and talented Casey DeSantis.

As the documentary rolled, there was silence in the theatre except for the gentle laughter as scenes from his early childhood flashed across the screen. Then the tears as Casey delicately told the story of the incident. Then the smiles as we all watched JT work his magic with JTTF recipients on the many deliveries he was able to make, a result of his dream of paying back the community that helped him. Then the wails as the story of his passing unfolded on the big screen.

One thing was evident throughout the film. It was JT's tenacity and his strong will and faith in God to live. Not just to live, but to thrive, and to make a difference in the world right from his wheelchair.

And, all the while to do it with grace and a smile and giving his God all the glory. All the things his Momma had taught him from the time he was a little boy.

It is no wonder the documentary received high acclaim. It was a true and perfect recounting of a life well lived.

Everyone left the theatre that day moved by not just the beautiful film, but the fact they had been able to witness this story unfold in person. A story that left a huge impression on them.

They would be better people because they had met JT Townsend.

It was wonderful how our family had embraced JT and his family … now our extended family. I thought back to the day we decorated Freedom House smiling as I envisioned our grandchildren Taylor and Abby with the glass cleaner bottle in hand and a roll of paper towels cleaning the windows. They were seven and nine, respectively, then. Time would tell how our relationship with this family would influence these little minds. I knew it would be good. We can talk till we are blue in the face about stewardship and helping others. Seeing the impact firsthand had to be the simplest form of understanding.

All this good had come from JT's dream. A dream to settle-up with the village that had stepped up to help him in his time of need. We sure couldn't stop now.

48

Another Angel—New Life and Death

IN 2008, LINDSAY ANNOUNCED SHE and her longtime friend Matt had taken their relationship to a new level. They were in love. This announcement prompted a wonderful courtship.

We loved Matt's quiet and sweet personality. He had a sort of calming effect on our once controlling and spirit-filled daughter. We admired his work ethic and his gentle spirit. We were thrilled when they became engaged. We loved their family and the strong values they held. They fit right into our crazy life immediately.

Matt had planned a serious proposal surprise. He told Lindsay they would be having a picnic lunch at the old fort grounds in St. Augustine, a favorite spot for them to enjoy many times before.

Many time, Lindsay and Matt had watched by-planes fly over the beach where they spent many long hours surfing and basking in the sun, enjoying time together. Lindsay mentioned she would like to fly in one of those stunt planes one day.

Remembering her request, Matt arranged for her dream to become a reality. He phoned one of the pilots out of the St. Augustine airport to give her a ride. He explained his idea was to propose to her through the headphones as she took her ride twisting and rolling in the sky on the flight of her life.

Well, the day was perfect, and the proposal came off without a hitch. They were married about a year later at our favorite venue TPC Sawgrass in the second wedding Tommy and I put on. It was an EPIC wedding to say the least and a fitting sendoff for our baby girl.

They settled into married life easily and we could not have been happier at her choice of a life partner.

One early fall day I had a strange request from Lindsay. Did I want to meet her at the Town Center for lunch? She rarely left her desk at Wounded Warrior Project. I wondered to what I owed this very special request.

We met at *Panera* where we chose a table outside in the delightful noon sun. She went in to place our order and I waited for her return. As she sat, she shoved her large purse toward me.

"Look inside," she said.

As I opened the leather flap, I could see several white pregnancy test sticks. I pulled one from the bag and read the results. It indicated she was pregnant.

I screamed in delight. "Could it be true?" she asked inquisitively.

"Well of course it could be," I replied.

"Well, I just don't believe it … that I am pregnant," she said.

I knew if we visited the local women's clinic, they would do a test and tell her immediately. We both got out our phones to locate the closest office and called to see if she could come in.

We drove to the office and after a few minutes it was confirmed.

"You are pregnant," said the nurse.

We hugged each other tightly and shed a few tears. It was super great news. She was in the very early weeks, so I agreed we needed to keep this under wraps until she had confirmed with the doctor.

As difficult as it would be to contain my excitement, especially with my dearest friends, I agreed.

What an amazing gift ... my little girl was having a baby. In true Lindsay fashion, all figured out, they had recently moved into a spacious home after living in a small condo for a couple of years. It was perfect timing. We hadn't been blessed with a grandchild for thirteen years. This was BIG!

It was suddenly October and my sixty-fourth birthday! Lindsay presented me with a beautiful photo she had taken of me kissing JT on the forehead at his college graduation reception with Carmen smiling down on us. It was a beautiful moment captured and I treasured the framed photo as I hung it on the wall in my bedroom, the first thing I would see when I opened my eyes each morning.

A few days after my birthday we received the call we had been dreading. Tom's Mother was nearing her passing from COPD she had battled for several years. We decided to make the trip to say our goodbyes.

Peggy had been such a blessing in the lives of Scott and I when we first met decades ago. I mean seriously, she never blinked an eye when her twenty-four-year-old young son was dating a thirty-three-year-old divorcee with a twelve-year-old son. In fact, she welcomed us with love and hugs. She was the example of what I wanted as a mother. We felt her love immediately and completely.

Tom and his sisters shared the many stories of life with a mom who stayed at home until they were teenagers. How she prepared the same meal depending on what day of the week it was. How each Saturday night their dad would take her out for a dinner date without the children. How she could not swim and was afraid of the water, yet, sat in the lounge chair next to the above-ground pool as they swam, and she soaked up the warm Cleveland summer sun. There were so many laughs. They were deeply loved and cared for, it was clear.

We were also able to share the news with her about Lindsay and Matt expecting a baby and she was elated.

Just a week or so after our visit she passed. Tom handled it quite well because he has a wonderful way of looking at the worst situations from the best vantage point. He had run this scenario through his mind many times before it happened. He prepared a eulogy that softened the blow of losing her, remembering the great laughs we all shared with this delightful woman. He shared how fortunate he was to have Peggy as his mother and what a great life she had made for their family and others.

Peggy and Lou had run the bingo game at Our Lady of Angels Catholic Church for over thirty years, supporting the Catholic school with the profits. They loved the game and became lifelong friends with the hundreds who would show up every week to play.

She worked for the City of Cleveland in the welfare department as a supervisor until retirement, helping families with their many needs.

Now, in her absence, Tom's Father, Lou would be watched over by his three sisters who lived within minutes from him. It would be difficult for Dad, losing his bride of fifty-five years. Tom had plans to bring his father down to Florida as many times a year as he would come to keep involved with all of the family near and far.

The holidays were approaching. We made plans to include the Cleveland family meeting up in New York City for Thanksgiving weekend. We had a great time.

Christmas came and went. I scheduled knee surgery for a torn meniscus just after the New Year. This was the first step in a series of events that would once again change our lives.

49

Life-Changing "CRHP"

THE YEAR HAD BEEN DIFFICULT losing both JT unexpectedly and Peggy. I was reluctant when approached by my dear friend Lauran to agree to attend a retreat at our church. It was called Christ Renews His Parish ... or CRHP. We agreed to attend together.

Tommy and I had been members of our parish for over twenty years, but we had never really participated, other than attending mass each Sunday.

The children had attended CCD classes required to receive their sacraments of reconciliation, first holy communion, confirmation, and marriage, but, truthfully, we could not tell you the names of any of the people who sat in the pews surrounding us for twenty years.

I completely believe God prepared me to accept Lauren's invitation to attend that weekend to prepare me further for what was lurking on my horizon.

Lauren and I discussed my guilt of being divorced and yet accepting the Holy Eucharist, which is not acceptable in our church. She wanted to help me right the situation. After the beautiful and inspiring weekend, I made an appointment with my new friend Deacon Dan who had been one of the staff for the retreat. Lauren even offered to go with me.

Sitting in front of this warm and caring gentleman whom I had just spent a spiritual weekend with, made me feel much more at ease as I laid my cards on the table wondering how he would react to my shame.

After I confessed what was bothering me, he rose from his desk, came around to me, and hugged me tightly saying, "We will fix this. Jesus loves you regardless of this and we are going to do whatever we need to do to correct this. I am going to help you."

Years of guilt seemed to wash away as I sobbed in his arms. It was out and I felt such relief.

It would take months to correct this situation, but it would be worth every minute.

50

Just Not Feeling Well

February 2014

M Y KNEE HAD BEEN BOTHERING me for several months. And hard as I tried, the pain just would not subside. I finally admitted I had a problem. The beach walking must have caught up with my aging bones.

Fred Funk had referred me to his orthopedic surgeon for a consult. After tests and an MRI, the doctor said it was a meniscal tear. He would go in, clean up the area, and then rehab for around six weeks. I scheduled the surgery for January 6th and prepared to be laid up for a while.

Lisa and Michele and I had been walking partners for as far back as we could remember being friends. These walks included what we referred to as therapy sessions. The miles would pass quickly as we shared what was going on in our most intimate lives. We would meet at my house and walk about four miles daily beginning early in the morning before the hot Florida sun would make it impossible, and of course, they also had to go to work.

Our girlfriends play such an important role in our emotional stability. Those daily walks and phone call conversations grew us closer and closer. We had become a trio of besties.

If we were facing a wedding or a class reunion or a reason to lose weight, we would up our game adding bicycle rides and walks on the beach. My body was beginning to show the signs of aging and my knees were the first part to go.

Six weeks after surgery I returned to the doctor for final instructions. He sent me to a physical therapist to begin rehab. I was eager to get back to my walking routine and missed the daily chats with my closest friends.

Several weeks into the sessions, I wasn't feeling very good. My PT asked me what was wrong. I truly could not explain it. I was fatigued and my stomach was upset. The more I pushed myself the worse I felt.

Tom called one day to let me know he was bringing someone home for dinner.

Since my two trips to Tuscany and the Italian cooking school, *Tuscookany* in 2010 and 2012, I was eager to prepare one of the wonderful recipes I had learned. I would pour a glass of cabernet, turn on Pandora to Andrea Bocelli, and begin the slow and methodical process that would fill the house with the fragrant smell of garlic and tomatoes. It was one of my favorite ways to relax.

I sat on the sofa and thought about what I needed from the grocery store. I really didn't feel I had the energy to go shopping, let alone prepare a meal.

When Tom came through the front doors with his friend, I was still sitting in the same spot on the sofa.

"What's for dinner?" he asked realizing the house didn't really smell like dinner was waiting.

"I just couldn't do it" I replied sadly.

"Well, let's all go grab a bite somewhere," he announced.

"You go ahead; I think I will go to bed," I replied.

Something was terribly wrong. This was not normal behavior for me. Tommy recognized it immediately.

That weekend we were invited to take pictures of our grandchildren at TPC. They were heading off to their first winter formal. We couldn't miss this. I gathered all my strength, and we made our way to the club.

Many of our friends were there to take pictures too. Some planned to have a bite to eat on the porch of the clubhouse and asked Tommy and me to join them.

Wine was poured and I stared at the glass. I just didn't care to drink a glass of wine let alone eat a meal. My stomach was upset. I felt as if my food was stuck just above my stomach. Something was wrong.

Tommy and I were both very healthy. We were seldom sick with even a cold. As a result, we didn't have a regular primary care physician.

But I had recently gone to one because I thought the prolonged use of ibuprofen prescribed by my orthopedic after surgery was affecting my stomach. I felt as if my food was not going down.

I have never been one to take medications I rarely finished the bottle of prescribed medications as we are always instructed. So, in my mind, it seemed logical that six or eight weeks of ibuprofen could influence my digestive system. All the warnings indicated this as a possible side effect.

The doctor had me report for blood workup and then sent the samples away for a very expensive analysis.

The report came back with no apparent problems indicated.

As I stared at my wine glass, one of my friends noticed.

"How long has it been that you have been feeling this way, Judi?" asked Lauren.

I explained my thoughts.

"You need to get an appointment at Mayo and get to the bottom of this. You look like you are losing weight too," she added.

"Yes, I've lost about fourteen pounds or more. And I'm not even trying."

Tom overheard the conversation and shared the dinner experience from the week before.

"Call Mayo and see if you can get in. It might take a few weeks, but you need to be seen there," Lauren stated emphatically.

And I knew she was right.

We knew it would be difficult to get an appointment with Mayo, so Tom and my son Louis spoke to our friend Dr. Kevin Kaplan who is a great orthopedic surgeon in the area and the team doctor for our Jacksonville Jaguars. He wanted to see me early Monday and would squeeze me in.

Monday morning came and I watched the clock until it read 8:30 AM. I phoned the appointment number for Mayo Clinic and reached a switchboard. I explained I needed to make an appointment and why.

The operator suggested I try a Mayo sports medicine doctor since my knee seemed to have caused the condition. I agreed and was connected to one of the outlying clinics.

"We happen to have a cancellation with a sport medicine doctor at 3:30 PM today, can you make that?" replied the nurse.

"Yes, absolutely I will be there." And I hung up the phone in disbelief knowing this must be God's divine intervention.

I headed over to Dr. Kaplan's office and he suggested more tests as my knee repair should have me feeling much better by now, even though he would have had me in PT much sooner. I explained I was going to Mayo for an appointment that afternoon. He agreed this would be good and he would follow up with the doctor to share his opinion

51

Diagnosis

Dr. Kristina DeMatas greeted me with a calm smile and began an examination as she questioned me about my symptoms. She was young and accomplished and had beautiful eyes that set me at ease right away.

"Let's do urine and blood samples today and we'll see where that leads us. I'll call you as soon as I have the results," she said.

Both samples were collected. I drove home thankful to have gotten that appointment and finally to be doing something about the problem.

Early the next morning Dr. DeMatas' office phoned asking if I could come right in for a sonogram. "Of course," I agreed.

As I lay on the table in the darkened room, I recalled how I had recently witnessed Lindsay's sonogram and the tiny baby that was growing within her tummy. That was such a positive reveal. I wondered what my report would tell, probably a gallstone or something, perhaps an ulcer. I really was not too worried.

The technician moved the probe across my abdomen making small clicks on the keyboard. She was measuring something. I asked her what that was.

"This is your liver and here is your pancreas," she replied, very nonplussed.

I knew marking the measurement could not be good, but the technician wasn't giving anything up.

"Your doctor will share the results once the radiologist has written the report."

When the examination was over. I drove home curious about the results but truly not that worried. I was happy I would be finding out what was going on and finally I felt confident Dr. DeMatas could do something for me.

I didn't expect to hear from the doctor until the next day; however, around 5 PM my phone rang. It was Dr. DeMatas office asking if I could come to the office and if my husband could accompany me.

That's odd I thought. "Yes of course," I replied.

I phoned Tommy at his office and told him he needed to come with me.

"What do you think that's all about?" he asked.

"Don't know what to think about it," I replied.

We both tried to imagine what could be wrong, but we could never have imagined what would be revealed at that appointment.

Tom has always said, "We are all just one phone call away from something life-changing." He had a predictable way of putting even our worst fears into perspective.

Dr. DeMatas entered the room and asked me to sit on the examination table. She tapped on my stomach several times as I winced in pain. She didn't seem surprised.

She turned to her monitor and began to relate the findings. Everything sounded normal until she pointed to a spot revealed by the sonogram. She turned the monitor so that we both could see it and suddenly she said…

"There is a mass in the head of your pancreas."

Tears began to slide down her cheeks as she spoke.

Suddenly Tommy leapt from the sofa to my side on the examination table.

"Could it be cancer?" Tommy asked.

"Most likely it is," she replied.

Tears began to form as Tommy held me.

"Can you live without your pancreas?" I asked.

"Yes, today you can, but you would be a diabetic," she answered.

We were both in shock with the worst news we had ever heard.

My mind kept repeating… *"You have a mass in your pancreas … most likely it is cancer."*

Dr. DeMatas handed us a card with a surgeon's names on it.

We have made an appointment for you to see Dr. Horacio Asbun at the Mayo Main Hospital tomorrow morning.

"Of course, we will be there," I replied.

In a few minutes, we were walking down the hall toward the exit of the clinic and back to Tom's truck as if we were looking down on our bodies from above.

Maybe it's not cancer, I kept repeating in my head. *Maybe it's something else.*

We dove to Chick-Fil-A and went inside to a table. Tom got our order and we sat at the table in shock.

"If you had a wish to do anything in the whole world, what would it be?" he asked.

"Honey, honestly, there is nothing. We have lived our lives like it was a continuous bucket list. There is nothing I want or anywhere I want to go," I answered.

We continued to talk about this shocking news.

We decided to wait till we spoke to the surgeon before we shared the dreadful news with the children. We needed to have something positive to give them and we hoped the surgeon would give us that information.

I don't recall if I slept that night. And I think we both were in some form of shock. I was like a zombie going through the motions, placing one foot in front of the other.

Regretfully, I did go online in search of something positive opposed to the gloom and doom of the deadly statistics that filled my mind with each mouse click. It was terrifying. I knew our children would do the same. We needed something positive.

52

Checking Into Mayo

A s we walked from the parking lot amongst the giant moss bearded live oaks that shed filtered sunlight on the sidewalk, we both were impressed by the magnitude of Mayo Clinic, Jacksonville. We located the hospital building and entered the sliding glass doors.

We found our way to the correct floor and office, checked in at the desk, taking a seat in the waiting area wondering what solution the surgeon would have for us.

Suddenly they announced my name.

We were escorted to an examination room and within a few minutes Dr. Horatio Asbun and his team entered the room. We were amazed with his good looks and warm demeanor. It was evident he understood our fear and trepidation and immediately put us as ease.

"So glad to meet you both today. We are going to see what we can do to help you with this frightening diagnosis," he said with his thick Chilean accent. "I know this is very difficult for you both. Now tell me what you are feeling," he asked.

Holding on to the hope that the mass discovered deep within my body was benign, I asked if it could be possible.

"Well, regardless, it must be removed. It has blocked your bile duct and is causing your body to be filled with bilirubin and the poisons that would normally run through your digestive tract," he explained.

He handed us a diagram and showed us what needed to be done.

"Only fifteen to twenty percent of patients with your condition are eligible to have this surgery. We would like to schedule it for Monday or Tuesday," he said.

It was called the "Whipple procedure" after the surgeon who developed it. It was an extensive nine-hour surgery that basically rerouted my digestive track. Recovery would be improved with his ability to perform the surgery medically known as a pancreaticoduo-denectomy laparoscopically. Few surgeons perform the surgery in this manner. The Whipple involves removal of the head of the pancreas next to the first part of the small intestine (duodenum). It also involves removal of the duodenum, a portion of the common bile duct, the gallbladder, and sometimes part of the stomach.

He made it apparent surgery was imminent and asked when I could be available.

Suddenly my thoughts raced to Lindsay and her impending due date just five days away. Not only that, but this was also "PLAYERS week."

For as long as we had lived in our home on Seven Mile Drive, we had thrown that weeklong party. Food had been ordered, and family would soon be arriving. How could we possibly throw in a nine-hour surgery and hospital stay.

The reality was beginning to eek its way into my mind. This was serious. I needed to have this tumor removed as quickly as possible.

"Well, let's take a moment here," said the doctor.

"The following week works better. Your daughter could have her baby on Tuesday, you could have The PLAYERS party in your backyard and invite all your family and friends. We could schedule the surgery for the following Monday. I will be there both pre – and post-surgical appointments. What do you say?" he asked.

"Do you think it is okay to postpone another week?" I asked.

"This tumor has been growing in your pancreas for many years, one more week is not going to make a difference. Go home, meet your new grandson, have your party and celebrate life," he answered.

We left his office with a definite plan, a folder filled with information about the procedure, and forms to complete for the hospital.

We now felt equipped with everything we needed to explain to the children Mom's possibility of having one of the deadliest forms of cancer. And of course, our plan of attack.

We slid into the truck and Tom drove directly to our church. As we made our way, we asked each other a million questions. But the most important one was, "How will we tell the children?"

Lindsay's due date was just six days away. This was supposed to be a joyful time for any family. And we had to give them this news.

We pulled into the parking lot of the church and fortunately the priests were in the sacristy.

We entered the sacristy where my friend Deacon Dan and Father Frank were removing their vestments after mass.

We shared the news with Deacon Dan, who had been helping me obtain an annulment, clearing the path for Tommy and I to be married in the Catholic church. He accepted the news as he hugged me tightly.

"We will immediately administer the sacrament of the sick," he said. As he opened his small prayer book to the correct page.

In the Roman Catholic church, the priest anoints the sick person's forehead and hands with holy oil in the form of a cross saying, "Through this holy anointing may the Lord in his love and mercy help you with the grace of the Holy Spirit. May the Lord who frees you from sin save you and raise you up."

Tears fell slowly down my cheeks. This was becoming real suddenly.

Tommy asked Father Frank if he could speak to him privately, as they moved to a small room just steps from Deacon Dan and me.

Deacon Dan continued to show me reassurance and let me know my church family would be walking right beside me every step of the way. He would check with me the next day.

After several minutes, Tom moved from the room with Father Frank to my side and grabbed my hand as we sat in a pew staring at the figure of Jesus Christ hanging over the altar in an empty church. We prayed for what seemed like a very long time until we were finished and stood to leave the church.

"I confessed to Father Frank I had not always been there for my wife throughout our marriage," Tom said. "He told me for my penance I was to lead my Mary and my family through this trial by emulating Joseph," he added.

From that moment on we have referred to each other as "Joseph" and "Mary" and wear medals that remind us. It was the perfect penance.

The children were aware we were going to the doctors and wanted an explanation of what was wrong with me.

Tom had scheduled a family meeting late afternoon and we headed to Lindsay's house where we were to meet.

Everyone was seated in the family room anxious to hear what this was all about. Tommy began and the tears started to flow.

I sat near Lindsay watching her reaction. My mother's instinct told me she was in a very fragile emotional state. I held on to hope that I appeared calm and together as their father explained about the surgery and how this would all unfold with his usual positive spin.

It all seemed surreal. I had always been healthy. I had always been in control. Suddenly within twenty-four hours, that had all changed. I was facing a life-threatening medical situation. My children and my husband would be there to support me, yet my future was uncertain.

After the family discussion, the children *Googled* pancreatic cancer and were terrified. Statistics showed only a five percent survival rate for five years. They all faced the possibility that their mom might not survive.

We left the house and headed home after an emotionally exhausting day. I slipped into bed. We finally managed to go to sleep.

Lindsay was going to the OB weekly in her final month. She explained to her doctor what was happening. The doctor agreed to induce her on her due date May 5th, if she didn't deliver before then. That way, Mom could meet her newest grandchild before she entered the hospital for the complicated and dangerous surgery.

Tom's father would be arriving on Sunday so he would also be here for the birth. It was his favorite week of the year, PLAYERS week. The delivery of his great-grandchild would be good medicine considering the bitter pill he would have to swallow when he received the news of his daughter-in-law's deadly diagnosis.

I shared the devastating news with my dearest friends Lisa and Michele. They were crushed but vowed to walk every stop of the way with me. We had been friends for twenty-plus years, sharing the many peaks and valleys of our marriages, our children's trials and tribulations, as well as the holidays and wonderful dinners and concerts and fun times. They were like sisters to me.

My sister Sherrie who lives in Arizona and my brother Ernie needed to be told. I made the phone calls and assured them both we had a plan. We were in good hands with Mayo and Dr. Asbun.

Feeling surprisingly well, it was hard to believe whatever it was growing inside my body could be so lethal. I seemed to be floating in a sea of uncertainty. The days were a blur, but I managed to put one foot in front of the other with my Joseph by my side. Once again, he had come to my rescue.

53

Baby Jude

Tom's Dad arrived as planned and we shared our news with him. He took it calmly but guardedly. We were happy to have his support even though we knew it would be difficult for him. We lightened the moment with news that Lindsay would be induced on Tuesday and his great-grandson would be making his debut.

Lindsay and Matt wanted to welcome their firstborn with just the two of them so they could bond for a bit as a new family unit. Having both sets of parents living so close was a blessing. The four of us waited patiently in the maternity lobby listening for the nursery chimes that rang out through the hospital, announcing another baby had arrived.

Fortunately, labor wasn't too difficult for Lindsay, and it wasn't long before Matt texted it was okay for all of us to come back to meet our newest little angel.

As soon as they were informed, they were having a little boy, they went to work deciding on the perfect name. They had a couple of names to choose from, and Lindsay loved the name "Jude."

There was a lot of discussion amongst the family and most of it not in agreement. Some felt it was too feminine a name for a boy. It was their child to name and it probably would be good advice for others not to share their name choices until the baby's arrival.

However, things had changed. The connection between Jude and my name Judi was undeniable. Tommy had always called me "Judes," so it made perfect sense to Lindsay to honor me in this special way.

"Meet Jude," announced Lindsay, as the four grandparents entered the room.

There was not one objection from that day forward about the name choice. We had no clue how this little guy would capture our hearts so completely, especially the heart of his namesake.

When it was my turn, I held this swaddled infant close to my cheek so I could take in his new baby scent. At that moment I let go of all the worry and concern I felt for myself and could only focus on this new life that God had given us.

Life is such a miracle. How can you not believe in God when you experience the birth of a new creation? I wondered if my daughter might finally grasp the depth of my love for her.

As a grandparent five times before this, I love each of my children deeply and completely. I felt this child was sent by God at this exact moment to be my little carrot. He would be one of the most important reasons for me to push on when I didn't have the strength to lift my head. I think everyone in the family understood this. Our hearts were filled with gratitude for this precious gift of life when what lay ahead of us was so uncertain.

54

Players Week

PLAYERS WEEK WAS UPON US and the traffic that poured into our small beach community was bumper to bumper. People flew in from all over the world to experience The PLAYERS at TPC Sawgrass and the beautiful Stadium Golf Course.

This event is unofficially considered the fifth major event of the PGA Tour golf calendar. Every PGA Tour professional who was fortunate enough to play this event was prepared and so was the TPC Clubhouse and grounds.

The head greens-keeper had worked the entire year to ready the course to its most favorable conditions.

The back of our home was prepared. Food filled every refrigerator in the house. A commercial ice refrigerator took up a good portion of the third bay of the garage. Two beautiful young bartenders stood in wait at the outdoor bar designed specifically for this one week of the year.

We were ready.

Wednesday, we had one more appointment with the surgeon to discuss what to expect day of surgery and after. The MRIs had been poured over and the surgeons who would be in attendance were prepared.

Unbeknownst to me, a team of doctors met Thursday at Mayo. This group of some of the finest doctors in the world, sit on what is called the "tumor board." They meet each week to discuss patients who have been newly diagnosed with serious cancers. These doctors are specialists in several fields. They review scans and each give their opinion on the course of treatment needed. Talk about a second opinion.

We had complete confidence in our surgeon and his team. We were told exactly what to expect the day of surgery and for the recovery period that could last a week in the hospital.

We left the building and headed back to the house where the crowd would be waiting.

We were on the JTB Bridge just five minutes from Mayo when my cell phone rang. It was Dr. Asbun.

"Where are you?" he asked.

"We are on the bridge heading back home," I replied.

"We need you to come back if you could please. We have something further to discuss with you," added Dr. Asbun.

We agreed, and Tommy headed back to Mayo as our curiosity piqued.

When we arrived at his office, Dr. Asbun had assembled his entire surgical team once more.

"It seems one of the residents found an image from the MRI that is quite concerning. It shows where your tumor has wrapped around your artery. This is a game-changer. The team recommends you cancel the surgery and begin chemotherapy to reduce the size of the tumor and perhaps shrink it so that it is not touching the artery."

"What are the chances of the tumor shrinking?" I asked.

"About fifty-fifty," was his reply.

I had mentally prepared for this dangerous surgery and believed it was important to remove this probable cancer from my body.

Tommy held me closely as Dr. Asbun conveyed, "This is a game-changer ... I would need to stint the artery and you could bleed out on the operating table."

Tommy looked at me and said, "I cannot make this decision for you honey."

I asked Dr. Asbun, "If I were your wife what would you do?"

"I am not afraid. I have done this once before eight years ago. I would do the surgery," he responded.

Every fiber in my body was telling me to get the tumor out. I prayed to God to give me the answer.

"Then let's get it out," I replied.

Dr. Asbun asked the residents in the room to make sure to say a prayer for Mrs. Zitiello before surgery on Monday. This was a shock to me but extremely comforting. My medical team would be praying for me. I knew I was in good hands now that we all understood God was included in my team.

We left the office again filled with anxiety and concern. Yet, I was sure the Holy Spirit had led me to make the right choice.

By Thursday I was beginning to feel the effects of the blocked bile duct. The whites of my eyes began to yellow. My skin took on a sallow appearance. I was also getting weaker.

The doctor had told me to listen to my body. I escaped to my room and tried to find some comfort in my bed.

Many of our good friends were coming by to share their concern with Tommy and hopefully to catch a moment with me.

Lindsay had brought baby Jude home from the hospital and thankfully she was feeling pretty good after her delivery. She instantly became the gatekeeper, allowing only my very best friends and my relatives just a few minutes with me.

In preparation for Jude's arrival, we had transformed Louis' old bedroom into a nursery complete with crib, dresser, changing table and rocking chair. A day bed was available for Lindsay and Matt should they want to rest when he was sleeping.

I was dehydrated and exhausted. With the tournament and festivities taking place right outside my door, I fought hard to make it to the scheduled surgery on Monday, but I was declining rapidly.

Calls were made to the doctor, and it was determined I would need a drain placed to remove the digestive fluid that had no clear path to where it was intended.

A procedure was scheduled for that afternoon and a drain was placed in the side of my stomach. Hopefully this would do the trick. But it would need to be checked, cleaned, and watched carefully.

I have little recollection of the next few days. I believe the drain was clogged and my fever began to soar. I was taken to the emergency room and paced on an IV for hydration. It was decided I should remain in the hospital for the weekend to build up my strength for surgery.

One of my best friend's sons had decided to create T-shirts to be worn on *Pink Sunday* at The PLAYERS in honor of those fighting cancer. The front of the shirt read *JUDES DUDES,* while the back read

JudiZ we love you. They even made one shirt especially for Tommy that read *JUDES MAIN DUDE.* On Sunday morning they all drove to Mayo and came to my hospital room in solidarity to encourage me before my surgery the next day. It was very touching, and the story and photo made the local newspaper of the *Jude's Dudes* at PLAYERS during the final round.

55

Surgery

SUDDENLY IT WAS MONDAY. I was being wheeled into the operating room.

When I shared with close friends my diagnosis, one of my dear friends who had gone through breast cancer came to visit. Marilee was a godly woman. In fact, her mother held some of the first Bible studies I had attended.

Marilee told me that she had found strength in Psalm 91. I had read it constantly since that day. This verse had given me great comfort.

"He shall cover thee with His feathers, an under his wings shall thou trust. His truth shall be thou shield and buckler."

As the nurses wheeled me away, my Joseph told me he loved me, and he would be waiting for me. I told him I was going to hide under Jesus' wing feathers. He smiled that beautiful smile I had fallen in love with and kissed me tenderly

I would not see him again for at least ten hours.

I am not certain what happened in the hospital waiting room, or who was there, except for Tom. I have been told most of my family and friends came and went, food was brought in, and prayers were said.

Dr. Asbun would report periodically to Tom on how the surgery was progressing.

Several of my CRHP sisters had met in the church for morning mass and stayed after to recite the rosary.

Thank God I had followed His prompting to attend CRHP and meet these wonderful sisters who would carry my requests directly to the only one who could answer them, my Lord and Savior Jesus Christ.

Sweet Jack, Lindsay's father-in-law, was also there with them, praying in silence.

My closest girlfriends were praying for me, wherever they were.

My Bible Study group had gathered at one of the homes and had prepared a list of scriptures and prayers they would say until they heard I was out of surgery.

It was comforting and completely humbling that so many would care enough to take time out of their lives to lift me up when I needed it most.

I was truly blessed.

When I came to, I felt as if I were in a white cocoon. I remember asking, "Am I in heaven?"

"No, you are right here with me," answered my favorite voice in the entire world.

I raised my hand to the Lord saying, thank you Jesus.

Tom rushed to my side and prayed over me thanking God that I had made it through the surgery.

Tubes, drains, blood pressure cuff, electrodes to measure my heart rate, oxygen, a catheter, an IV, and a morphine pump were hooked up to me. I was aware of the pain in my torso. I pushed the button on the pump and felt immediate relief. Several hours passed and finally Dr. Asbun and his surgical team appeared.

After checking me over and reading my chart, he proclaimed enthusiastically, "Well my dear, at this moment you are cancer free. I have done my part, now the rest is up to you."

I believe God saved my life, but that day Dr. Asbun acted as His hands. How could I ever thank this man who used the God-given skill to successfully complete a nine-and-a-half-hour surgery that would save my life?

The nurses came in to check my connections and update the laptop that recorded the readings, my administered meds and outputs.

The nurses assigned to this floor are absolute angels. They deal with such difficult cases and do so with compassion and tenderness. I fell in love with every one of them as they cared for me and came and went on and off shifts.

And my sweet Joseph ... slept on a sofa in my room every single night I was admitted. He never left my side. He barely slept because all night the nurses came and went turning on the lights and checking me consistently every hour or so.

Again, it is not clear who visited and when, but I am sure my sweet children were the first to come. I bet it was frightening to see me all hooked up and puffy from being blown up for the laparoscopic surgery. I had to be a sight. But with the help of my medications, I truly didn't care. I was alive ... that was all that seemed to matter.

I have a beautiful picture of the sacred heart of Jesus that I have carried for maybe fifty years. Whenever there is anything troubling happening, I have prayed over that picture. It has given me immense strength. Before I left for the hospital, I made a copy of it and when I was able, I asked Tom to tape it to my IV stand. Jesus' soft, warm eyes gazed at me constantly. I love that image to this day.

The second day after surgery I was told I had to sit in a chair. While it was difficult, I knew I had to do this so that I could work my way to being released to go home. The next day, I was instructed to walk the hall to the nursing station with the help of a stand sort of walker. Someone would accompany me pushing my IV along. Each day I was required to walk further and more often. Each day more and more of my tubes and hook ups were removed.

My oldest grand-daughter, Taylor, was graduating from high school during my hospital stay. Much to my delight she showed up in her cap and gown, bringing me a bouquet of beautiful bright sunflowers on her way to her graduation ceremony. I was beyond delighted as tears of gratitude streamed down my face. I had been sad not being able to attend.

Friends came and visited. It wasn't long before Dr. Asbun and his team agreed I could go home. (five days only since surgery!)

Lindsay had brought baby Jude to the hospital one time, but it was not a very good place for a newborn to be with all the germs around. So, I was happy to get home to my own bed and to be able to see him.

The drains that worked to remove the ascites, a fluid buildup near my bile duct, were still in place from before the surgery. They were uncomfortable and made it difficult to move. But while my stomach appeared to only have a few small incisions, the inside was where most of the healing was taking place.

The plan was to allow a few weeks to recover from surgery, then to begin my treatment, a regimen of chemotherapy and radiotherapy that would continue until the end of December to take care of any microscopic cancer cells. Pathology had determined the tumor was indeed adenocarcinoma and there were five out of thirty lymph nodes testing positive for the cancer as well. Because the tumor extended out beyond my pancreas around the artery, I was Stage 3. It would be important to begin treatment as soon as I could.

Home for almost a week and struggling to gain my strength back, a fever took over. The doctor was called and told me to get to the ER immediately. As soon as we arrived, my team was checking me over and it was determined, as with fifty percent of Whipple patients, I had contracted an infection.

Admitted back into the hospital, I remained for twenty-one days. Now, an infectious disease doctor took charge, Dr. Brumble. I was put on four of the most effective and potent antibiotics. While the heavy-duty drugs fought the infection, they further weakened my already enervated body. I was sent home with orders for home health care to visit me twice daily to administer the IV antibiotics and report my vitals to Dr. Brumble.

Administering the IV antibiotics was a minimum four-hour process twice a day confining me to bed. They also affected my taste buds, suppressing my declined appetite further. Nothing tasted good and I didn't want to eat.

At one point, Tom wanted me to drink supplement drinks to give me the calories I needed to regain my strength. Once again, I could not force them down. The situation was grim, but at long last, the infection subsided, and the antibiotics were no longer required.

Now began the difficult journey to regain strength. I needed to rejuvenate my body to prepare it for cancer treatment. Time was critical.

Lindsay stepped into action pushing me to get out of the bed and walk with the stroller holding our most precious cargo, baby Jude, around the natural area just beyond our house. She was a loving and persistent force behind my recovery from the infection and healing from surgery. She encouraged me to eat, move, and get out of bed. If not for Lindsay, I would have continued to decline and perhaps even been put on a feeding tube. I will be forever grateful for her persistence.

There is nothing like the love between a mother and daughter.

56

Post-Surgery Treatment

T HE IDEA OF CHEMOTHERAPY IS daunting. Before your first
infusion, you and your caregiver are required to watch a video
explaining what to expect. As that first infusion is hooked up, you
watch curiously as the clear liquid your oncologist has prescribed drips
into the plastic tubing attached to your port access and makes its way
through the chambers of your heart and through your body in search
of the cancer cells it is intent on destroying.

Tears filled my eyes as the first few drips entered my body. I had
already received a bag of fluids and anti-nausea meds via the port. But
now the drugs were entering my body, hunting down my silent killer.
While it was frightening, it was crucial to my continued existence.

In the beginning I would receive a fairly easy form of chemo—
Gemcitabine. The six-week scan would determine if it was doing what
was expected. The side effects were minimal, my hair did not fall out. I
did not feel nauseous to where I was confined to bed. And it appeared
to work. My scan showed no additional masses, nodes, or tumors.
Chemotherapy treatments lasted four weeks.

Now on to radiotherapy and the "mask."

It looks rather like a coat of armor when you see it for the first time, just a thick plastic mesh that is softened during what is called the "assimilation" appointment. The form is sculpted to the body at the radiation site. Ironically it reminded me of something worn by a super-hero, or maybe a gladiator.

The form would be kept in the radiation room and each day when I came for treatment, the techs would position it and aim the radiation device to the specific spot the CT scans determined needed radiation.

The first day I was asked if I approved of having radiation tattoos. The tech explained it made it easier for them to line up the device. I replied immediately, whatever you like. They proceeded to pen small blue dots on my torso.

As the needle pierced my skin I flinched. It was far more painful than I had anticipated. But I thought…It's just a tattoo…lots of people get far more than a few blue dots. I tried hard to control the apparent discomfort. Finally, the techs decided not to subject me any further.

"We'll be fine with what we have so far, you don't need to do this."

Each morning when I arrived for my treatment, I would lay on the radiation table and place my hands above my head grabbing two metal handles. Under my knees, the kind and gentle radiation techs would place a wedge and then they would strap my feet together so they could not move. They would wrap me in a warm white blanket from the top of my legs down, then place the mask over my torso and turn my body ever so slightly with their cold hands until the markers that were tattooed on my stomach matched up to the markers on my mask. (They always apologized for their hands being cold!)

It felt as if I were completely restrained as they secured the locks on my mask to the table. I thought to myself, if I gained more than a few pounds, they would have trouble getting this to lock, but of course that was not an issue these days. I could not move an inch.

The techs would exit the room, asking me if I was OK. They would shoot an X-ray to be certain my organs were in the perfect position to receive radiation. Some days a slight correction was needed, and they did this remotely. The table would move a touch until I was in target range.

Once I was in position, the radiation machine would orbit the table twice. There was no sound. A large sign the shape of an EXIT sign, reading "BEAM ON" filled the darkened room with a red glow. It reminded me of something from Star Trek ... like "Beam me up Scotty" or something. But I am sure it is just a warning to anyone entering the room.

There was no pain at all, only a warming of the area being radiated as I lay secured to the table. And the only physical effects were some "browning" of my skin and a little swelling and tenderness of the organs internally.

While laying, there I would tell Jesus thank you for another day of life and another step to my healing while I lay there for approximately five minutes listening to Pandora's *French Cafe* by personal request.

While it didn't appear on the outside of my body that the radiation was harming me, my oncology PA described the inside of my radiation area as "raw meat." The radiation burned the insides and destroyed muscle seeking out any possible cancer cells in its path.

Near the end of radiation therapy, I felt weak as I changed into my gown for treatment. As the radiation techs strapped me into place below the large external beam radiation machine, they agreed I needed to see the doctor. The doctor said there was no reason I shouldn't take the treatment. I was so close to the finish line. We had to proceed. I put on my big girl panties and headed toward the radiation room.

On the morning of my twenty-eighth and final radiation treatment, the girls asked me if I wanted to take my mask with me or if they should throw it away. For some odd reason I felt like I needed to take the mask with me, like it was part of my journey. I couldn't think of having it thrown in some random hospital trash bin. It was such a big part of my life for the past twenty-eight treatments. So, I brought it home in a hospital plastic bag that read "personal belongings."

Months later, I walked the mask out to the garbage can and chucked it in. I was ready to be done with it.

Finished...

It was back to the chemotherapy suites.

Three months later, in the midst of chemotherapy I received a call from a friend, the editor of a small local beach town magazine.

She explained the November "giving" issue features local philanthropists and she wanted to do an article on our family.

We have never been ones to seek out a pat on the back for what we have done to help others, so I politely said "no" and my family agreed we should not make any kind of public statement about our philanthropic work.

My friend persisted. I could tell the story in my own words. This got me thinking.

There had been so many God whispers in my life. Things that happened that burst open the next door that would have been missed had not the last thing occurred. My Bible studies had given me a new point of view. I was piecing together so many events from my past that seemed to follow a definite design. One square of the quilt leading to the next. I was finally realizing God had been behind everything. And, the more I thought about it, the more I recognized it.

It is never easy to share God stories with others, not really knowing their own beliefs. They may not see the chain of events so clearly originating from a God who had a plan for my life mapped out before I was even conceived. And would someone in mainstream media allow me to suggest God was the orchestrator?

I doubted it.

But it was worth a shot.

Sitting at my computer, I dashed off an email to my friend explaining what I wanted the piece to be about and waited for her response.

She said, "The article is about you and your family. Your faith is what your family is all about. Anyone who knows you has to agree with that. What you describe is exactly what the article will be about."

Within days, a writer called me to interview me. She was kind and introspective. I felt comfortable sharing how we had started years ago giving to families at Christmas time. How we would take our small children the week before Christmas to the houses and set the wrapped gifts in their home. We also gave a card and gift card to help pay for a holiday meal. And, on the drive home, we were tearful sharing the thoughts that we each had about how blessed we were to be able to do this for a deserving family. That was the impetus for what was to become a lifetime of giving.

The interview was moving along nicely until she asked me a simple question. "Tell me about the next JT Townsend Foundation event."

Tears welled up in my eyes and I tried not to let her notice through the phone that I was crying. She had taken me by surprise. Since my illness, there had been no fundraising events. The friend who was keeping the office running could not handle fundraising along with everything else the job required.

Applications were coming in weekly and the checkbook was slowly emptying.

"I'm sorry, did I say something wrong?" she asked.

"No, it's just since I have been sick, we have not been able to do any fundraising. We have applications but the money is running out to fill them," I replied.

"Well, how much money do you need to fill the applications you have right now?" she asked.

We had about twenty applications for $50,000 pending. I phoned her with the information. She told me to give her an hour.

Within an hour she and a gentleman showed up on my doorstep. The man was her fiancé. I invited them in and after introductions, they handed me a check for $50,000 to cover the applications.

The gentlemen's daughter had gone to high school with JT Townsend, knew the whole story, and had seen the wonderful things JT had been able to do for others who were in the same position he had found himself in after his incident. They felt moved to help.

Tears once again filled my eyes as we hugged, and I thanked them for their generosity.

Later that night I thanked God for bringing them into my life in such a big-hearted way.

When the article came out, I was pleased I had listened to His prompting. The article was not so much about us, it was about how our faith in God had led us to be able to help so many others. It was exactly what I had hoped it would be. Just another in the ever-increasing number of God whispers we had experienced.

The four more months of chemo following radiation were actually pretty tolerable. I was still losing weight and somewhat weak, fighting through it. On December 24th, 2014, I walked out of Mayo's chemo floor smiling, my treatment completed.

For thirty-one years, Tommy and I had thrown a Christmas Eve party. This party had become tradition for many of our friends and neighbors and certainly for our family. This was the only year we opted to let Lindsay and Matt throw the party. And it was a beautiful and wonderful gesture on their part to maintain the tradition for our family and friends.

Tom and I headed home a bit earlier than midnight and we prepared the presents for the next morning. It was a beautiful Christmas after all.

57

Life Goes On...

Six weeks after I finished my treatment, I was scheduled for a CT scan to determine if there had been any more nodes appear. The first scan was clear and the second. My oncologist suggested we go to two-month scans, and we agreed.

One thing that became abundantly clear ... I no longer saw any value in the things I had considered to be so important. When you face death, objects become nothing in the grand scheme of things. The Bible instructs us not to worship false idols. The Waterford crystal on display in my lighted cupboards, all gifts from Tom's parents, didn't seem to sparkle as bright. They were just things. I had learned what holds true value in our life on earth. It's our family whose eyes light up when they look at you. It's the loving touch of your best friends as they sit for hours on your bed and rub cream on your feet to make you feel just a little better. It's the loving prayers of your husband that we could accept God's will no matter what it was. Those are the treasures to behold.

I enjoyed having baby Jude at the house each day, witnessing every milestone. It was as if God had sent this little child to be my carrot, to keep me striving to heal and get stronger. We had developed a solid and very special bond.

When he would arrive in the morning, we would play music videos. *Somewhere Over the Rainbow* was his favorite. He would watch intently smiling.

Tom admitted he would leave the house for work after seeing this and shed tears of joy. It was a very special time.

Life continued for not only Tommy and me, for our children too.

Louis had found his soulmate and proposed Thanksgiving Day. Emily was a nurse in the ER at one of the big hospitals downtown. She was beautiful and accomplished and they dated for three years.

He had arranged for Lindsay to capture the moment at the beach. "Bernie", their Bernese Mountain Dog completed the picture as Louis dropped to his knee and asked the magical question. She said "yes." We knew it would be a party-filled year ahead as they formulated their wedding plans.

When I was at my weakest point just after my Whipple surgery, Tom had asked me if I had any places I wanted to go or things I wanted to do when I recovered. I told him in that moment I would love to take our entire family to my favorite place on the planet, Italy. Share the beauty I had discovered with all the children and grandchildren. He promised as soon as my treatments were finished, and I was strong enough to travel and walk, we would go. The trip was being planned for ten days, in July.

"We are traveling to the most romantic place on earth in July … all of us together … why not get married in Lake Como?" I suggested when the conversation turned to a wedding date and location that weekend.

The future bride and groom looked at each other and smiled. They liked the idea. It would take a lot of work to get the church to approve the nuptials and travel plans would need to be agreed to by Emily's parents too, but it all seemed dreamlike.

This gave everyone something positive to be thinking about and working on in the months to come. Louis and Emily made an appointment with the Deacon at our parish and Lindsay, Tom, and I began our search for the perfect Lake Como waterfront villa to house all fifteen of us. Airfare was shopped. Transportation would be required with a driver. Passports were acquired down to our smallest traveler Jude who was going to be just fourteen months when we embarked. We even hired a wedding planner in the small nearby town of Bellagio. It was exciting and the entire family joined in the planning.

My stamina was improving as I focused on watching little Jude and looked forward to his arrival at my door each day. In the beginning, once Lindsay went back to work, we hired a nanny to care for him at my house in case I wasn't up to it. I was not supposed to lift anything over ten pounds as my insides were healing from the surgery and radiation. The nanny was a huge help as Jude began to become mobile.

The eight-week scans were coming back stable, meaning no evidence of new nodes, tumors, or spots that could be suspect. We were in a good place.

Louis and Emily, with the help of the wedding planner had found a fourteenth-century gothic cathedral, The Church of San Giorgio, located across the lake from our villa in the small town of Varenna. The priest would perform the marriage ceremony in a traditional wedding mass. The approval of our local diocese was required in order for the vows to be recognized in the Catholic Church. All of the formalities were completed. We were ready to go.

A mahogany Chris Craft type boat, adorned with white flowers on the bow, was chartered to take the groom and his groomsmen across

Lake Como to beautiful Varenna, a twenty-minute boat ride. The boat would return to the villa to pick up the bride and her maids.

There would be a short walk from the boat dock up steps to the piazza where the townspeople would congregate. This was a popular wedding destination, and the locals would gather and cheer as they watched the bridal parties enter the beautiful cathedral and emerge as husband and wife.

Everything we could possibly think of had been arranged, down to photographers. We were all extremely excited for the week to arrive, and finally it was time.

The week was filled with fun as each day's plan unfolded. There was plenty of time for shopping, a quick train to Milan, eating out, exploring Bellagio and the beauty of Lake Como.

The July temperature was very warm. It felt exhilarating to bathe in the cool waters of Lake Como. We gazed across the measureless water to the Swiss Alps on the other side. From our vantage point, it seemed that toy trains twisted and turned their way through the mountains disappearing into tunnels only to emerge in a few minutes at the other side continuing on their way. It was truly surreal.

The wedding was out of a fairy tale book. It was the perfect way to begin a life together. Their marriage had been blessed by a wonderful Italian priest. The rest was up to them.

After the ceremony we all sauntered back to the boat dock where a larger boat was waiting to take us on an hour-long ride around Lake Como toasting with prosecco and noshing antipasti as the photographer captured amazing moments. Back at the villa, a chef was preparing a celebratory meal in the garden.

We were making the sixty-meter walk from the boat dock back to the villa with the bride and groom along the narrow shoulder of the road leading to our villa gate when a car stopped next to us.

"Judi?" shouted a woman I recognized, in a thick Italian accent.

"Laura?" I shouted back.

It was Laura Giusti, the first chef who had taught my Tuscookany Mediterranean Cooking Class at Casa Ombuto five years before. We had remained Facebook friends and messaged each other or emailed news to stay in touch. On my second cooking vacation to Torre del Tartuffo, just three years before, Laura had made a point to visit me, joining us at dinner and meeting the friends I had brought along.

We invited Laura and her friend to come to the villa for a drink and to meet the family. They did so and we enjoyed an hour together catching up. The encounter was yet another God whisper. How could she be traveling on a remote road from Milan to Bellagio at the precise moment I was walking that same road? I treasure the picture the photographer captured of us hugging each other in disbelief.

Emily and Louis spent their honeymoon night in a beautiful hotel in Bellagio. Emily took a picture with her phone out her window in the morning of two swans swimming in the lake below.

You just can't make this stuff up!

The fact that I was alive after such a diagnosis just fifteen months before was miraculous. Our strong faith and that of our friends who prayed for us had brought us to this enchanting destination. God had given me the strength to make it this far, and, to the best of our knowledge, cancer-free. It was almost unbelievable.

At times I wondered if I were dreaming. I even asked Tom, my Joseph, "Am I already in heaven?"

He would smile at me with that beautiful smile and say, "I thank God each morning for the blessings He has given us."

58

Joseph and Mary

OUR LOVE HAD DEEPENED DURING this trial. I had heard of other couples whose marriages had crumbled in the face of catastrophe. But not ours. In fact, Tommy would tell me lovingly, "I feel giddy, I am so in love with you."

What woman on this earth doesn't want to hear those words?

And my Joseph didn't just talk about his love for me. He expressed it in a million ways. He never missed a doctor's appointment, scan, or test. He sat at my side through everything. But the most amazingly loving thing he did was to pray over me.

We had a routine, as we would approach the turn into Mayo Clinic, he would grab my hand and ask God for strength to handle whatever would be revealed or endured this day. We didn't pray for the cancer not to return, we prayed for God's will and the courage and strength to handle whatever would be revealed.

I felt it was the greatest expression of his love. And, honestly, I could not have faced this whole illness without this strong faith he displayed that gave me courage every step of the way.

Our faith had brought us through the biggest storm of our lives. And even though uncertainty lay ahead. I believed we could endure anything with God guiding us and in our hearts.

No longer did I pray for a few minutes in the morning or at night, I held full on conversations all day and night with Jesus. Aware, He was walking in my shadow, my dearest comrade, every step, every moment of every day. I felt peaceful and assured I could face anything that was thrown my way. I had my faith, I had my husband, my children, and my friends. I knew how blessed that was and how grateful I was for His favor.

One day I received a call from Deacon Dan. He had been working diligently on the paperwork required to annul my previous marriage and allow Tom and me to be married in the Catholic church. My case had been pled to our diocese leaders and we were cleared to be married in the church. This was the day I had prayed for.

It would be a small private wedding ceremony held in the beautiful side altar at our parish. The room held about twenty people, just big enough for our growing family and my closest friends.

I found a beautiful ivory dress that would look beautiful with my precious pearl necklace and earrings. A date was set.

The day of the ceremony, our family arrived at the church along with my dearest friends. Lisa had bought me a bouquet made up of beautiful purple Cala Lilly. We assembled in front of the small altar, our children as witnesses, as Deacon Dan performed the ceremony that would make our union official in the eyes of the Catholic church.

Amazingly, the one act of my Grandmother Kathy when I was just six weeks old, baptizing me, had been a strong factor in the church granting me dissolution of my previous marriages. I was indeed a

Catholic my entire life, but never knew this view of the church until I was sixty-five years old.

No longer would I need to feel the guilt I anguished over when I took holy communion. That part of my life had been forgiven and any sin erased by the sacrament of reconciliation. Not only was I now officially a Catholic, but our marriage was blessed by the church family that had taken me under their wings. It was one of the most beautiful memories in my lifetime.

Lauren and Deacon Dan had unlocked the door that had kept me locked up in a guilt-filled room most of my adult life. For that I am eternally grateful.

And my love for Tom was deeper and stronger; I knew we could face anything together.

59

Sharing the Story

WHEN I BEGAN THIS JOURNEY, my friends suggested I journal about it. I had been told I had a propensity for writing. My first trip to cooking school with Kelly, I journaled each day sending the pages home to share my trip with Tom and the children. When I returned home, I decided to start a blog. The first entries were of my week in Poppi, Italy, at Casa Ombuto, then recipes I would prepare with photos of the plated meal, then life experiences, and even a page for things I had learned in my life. It was a passion I enjoyed.

Writing about this pancreatic cancer voyage was a source of relief for me. I would share my blog posts on social media. It became a way to update my friends without having to repeat my story constantly.

Then another wonderful door was opened. My Mayo doctors began to give my name and number to newly diagnosed patients. I knew the feelings they harbored deep within even if they didn't communicate them. I would share my experiences with surgery, chemotherapy, and radiation. We would discuss the fear of the CT scan, what we named "scanxiety." Bonds were developed as I kept a journal of names and numbers and notes on where they were in their treatment.

Friends around the country would call me to ask if they could share my number with a newly diagnosed patient with pancreatic cancer who might be a friend or relative. I agreed immediately to speak with them.

We were a diverse group spread across the globe. We shared a common connection. I always asked about their faith and would explain the role my faith had played in my acceptance of this death sentence. I agreed to have been terrified at first just as they were. But I had found peace.

Not everyone had a support system. These were the people I felt most concern for. Not only did they perhaps not believe they may not have anyone to go to appointments with them, to be sure they ate, walked, drank water, took medications. Some had no caregiver. And probably nobody to pray for them.

My first question to each caller was, "How is your faith?" If it had been years since they had been in church, get plugged in once again. Their church family could be a huge source of help for them. And they would receive the prayers they needed.

My journal of PC warriors was filling up. I would follow up with a text, email, or a phone call occasionally. Sometimes, I would find out they had passed, "earned their purple wings…" as we say. When I discovered this, I would highlight their information and include the date they died. Half the names in the journal were highlighted. This was the grim reality of pancreatic cancer. It pushed me forward. It made me appreciate every breath I took, day I saw the sun rise and set, weeks and months and even years passing. For some reason God had graced me with strength and promise to go on. But I felt a need to do more.

A local chapter of Pan-Can (Pancreatic Cancer Action Network), headquartered in California, had reached out to us during my treatment asking us to join them to raise awareness and funding for PC.

They had a support arm offering answers to questions a PC patient might have. The website is informational and stresses the importance of funding for this deadly cancer that has not been given much attention. The survival rate was just five years from diagnosis. The treatment oncologists offered were designed for other cancers such as breast and lung. But, truthfully not very effective.

Pancreatic cancer statistically presents when it has already progressed to Stage 3 or 4, leaving treatment options extremely limited.

This twenty-year-old organization, PanCan.org, was in a fight to find research funding from the NIH and the rich Federal Defense budget that then President Clinton had tapped into as he declared war on not another nation or group that threatened, but a war on cancer.

They hold organized walks with chapters around the nation called "Purple Stride" to raise not just funding but also awareness for this fight that had been for years considered to be a lost cause.

My husband, family, and friends considered this a perfect opportunity to band together to form another group, "Jude's Dudes." Purple T-shirts were ordered with our team-name on the front and "We love Judi Z," printed on the back.

That year we had over one hundred runner/walkers. Tom organized brunch around our pool for all of our team after the race. It was an amazing love fest that I will never forget.

Tommy and I also participated in Pan-Can's advocacy program. We flew to Washington DC taking Abby, our teenage grand-daughter, along. During the weekend we met other survivors from across the country and sat in on many clinical presentations learning about pancreatic cancer and what is being done to fight it at this time.

After an insightful Sunday, we planned our strategy to meet with our local congressmen and senators to ask them to join our quest to get their endorsement for federal funding.

We learned so much and we met so many people who shared our passion. There were even eight survivors. Most were under a year or two from diagnosis, but there were two over ten-year survivors. This was encouraging.

Something had to be done about the low five-year survival rate. So much had been discovered about breast cancer. What could we do to bring awareness and research to this lethal cancer that was affecting almost sixty thousand Americans each year? That number represents more Americans than those who die in automobile accidents. How could this be?

60

Champions for Hope

A FEW WEEKS AFTER THE TRIP, Tommy came to me with a very interesting idea.

"You know how I have always wanted to throw a golf tournament at TPC Sawgrass?" he questioned.

"Yes," I answered quizzically.

"Well, I think we should put together an event that would be able to raise funds to help JTTF and funding for pancreatic cancer research," he said excitedly.

"We have so many friends in business and locally, I am sure they would consider corporate donations and even personal ones," he added.

"One epic annual event that could fund both causes."

I could see the wheels turning and the excitement building.

I loved the idea. We had made many friendships not only here in our small beach community, but throughout the country with our business.

This idea suddenly grew legs.

The more we spoke to people, the more we discovered others who had a friend or a relative who had been touched by pancreatic cancer. It was incredible. And, the best part, they all wanted to help.

Over the next few months, we formed a new foundation along with our old friends Fred and Sharon Funk, Funk–Zitiello Foundation. We incorporated and applied for nonprofit status as a 501c3. We reached out to Mayo Clinic to help us find promising research projects we might fund. We had a business plan and a passionate group to help us.

This would be no ordinary golf tournament. This would be a two-day event to be held at one of the most prestigious venues in the country, TPC Sawgrass, and golf of course on the TPC Stadium course.

Fred got to work inviting fellow pro-golfers. I reached out to the Jacksonville Jaguars who had such a deep connection to JT Townsend when he was alive.

We would throw a celebrity golf tournament pairing each foursome with a pro-golfer or an NFL player.

Tommy wanted it to be a charity tournament like none other. He dreamed of having a food or beverage vendor on every other hole. And all of this would be donated.

We met with Bill Hughes, the GM of TPC Sawgrass and his team of directors, and willingly started putting the event together.

The JTTF board members were happy to volunteer, knowing this would enable them to fundraise and keep JT's foundation helping the disabled.

Everyone we met with seemed as excited and as vested as we.

Our JTTF marketing board member, Pauline Gerry, put together a first-class marketing package and came up with the name, *Champions for Hope Celebrity Golf Classic*. (Champion from the local

Emmy-nominated documentary, *CHAMPION the JT Townsend Story* that Casey DeSantis and First Coast News had written and produced, and Hope as a perfect word for pancreatic cancer warriors.)

It was perfect!

A first-class venue was expensive, we would be required to pay a hefty price. This prompted Tommy and I to come up with a budget large enough to produce the amount of net income we needed to fund three very promising research projects for early detection of pancreatic cancer and a significant amount to JTTF for their ever-increasing requests for adaptive equipment and financial assistance for the disabled community.

We operated quite differently than other charities. We had no paid employees and no overhead. We approached each expenditure looking for ways to have that line item donated. To others surprise, it worked. We personally paid for as much as we could, and many companies donated whatever we needed from them to make this event a one-of-a-kind experience.

A local philanthropist and friend had a personal connection to pancreatic cancer and helped us vet out the three research projects. He offered anonymously to put up $230,000 and challenged us to match this; $500,000 was needed to set up research at Mayo Clinic, Jacksonville.

Another local pancreatic cancer nonprofit agreed to pitch in $70,000 to help us reach our goal.

We needed to net $200,000 for Mayo and $150,000 for JTTF to achieve what we dreamed we could do.

The first annual event was inspiring and lived up to the adjective Tommy had described ... EPIC.

"This is a proverbial love fest," Tommy exclaimed as he spoke from the heart to two hundred and sixty guests attending the gala the night before the tournament.

The first annual event exceeded our expectations, netting over $650K.

We immediately went to work, imagining how we could top the event the next year.

Champions for HOPE was launched and our dreams were coming true. A movement had been born out of a lethal diagnosis and the passing of a young man with big dreams and a strong faith.

We gave the entire glory to God. Tommy and I both agreed this was our calling. God had given us this trial and this additional time for me to make big things happen for our two deserving passions. He had been preparing us our entire lives for this moment in time. And we would take no credit ourselves.

This was just another miracle, along with my continued good reports amidst a less-than-optimistic cancer diagnosis.

God continued to lead us, and the gift was … we were following.

61

The Rest of the Family

SCOTT AND BLAKE'S FOUR CHILDREN, our older grands, were thriving since moving to Ponte Vedra Beach several years before my cancer diagnosis. They were deeply enmeshed in PV Softball. Scott had even taken a coaching position. Taylor, Abby, Tommy, and Olivia were committed athletes working hard to perfect their skills.

Scott was working as an account rep for a national health and beauty aid company. When they moved closer to us in 2003, Taylor and Abby were in elementary school, the twins attended Pre-K.

With Blake's teaching background she was able to secure a teaching position at the preschool covering the twin's tuition. This was a great financial help to this growing family.

Scott and Blake had found a great home just a fifteen-minute drive from our house that had four bedrooms, dining, and family rooms and a bonus room on a large pie-shaped lot on a cul-de-sac. It was perfect for them, and we were happy to have our family nearby. We could finally host the Sunday family dinners we had always dreamed of.

Lindsay and Matt had found a great home just five minutes from our house that needed some TLC shortly before Jude was born. The house had plenty of room for a growing family. It was fun to decorate the mid-century ranch and we made it a family project. They were so happy.

Louis and Emily had found a great house in our neighborhood. It was the perfect starter home and one they could fill with children. Louis was working for Tommy at our now family business. Emily was in nursing school and working as a microbiologist at Mayo Clinic. They were doing great.

Evan, Tom's son from a prior relationship, had moved from Cleveland to Clearwater during high school with his family shortly before we moved to Ponte Vedra Beach.

We had had no contact since around age twelve, when he had called to ask Tom if his mom's new husband could adopt him. Tom assured his young son he would always be his dad regardless of the adoption should he ever need anything. He explained, at this mother's prompting, he needed a full-time dad in his life. And the adoption took place.

Evan's mother believed it was important for him to have a father in his life and rightfully so. We always left the door open, another thing I admired about my husband. After all, he had taken Scott into his heart and loved him like his own. I too accepted Evan.

When Evan was in his mid-twenties, he reached out to Tommy once again. We both made it clear we were there for him, wherever the relationship would take us. And Evan was welcomed by all as one of the family.

Tommy and my life were complicated by the many decisions and consequences we faced over decades. And, considering how things could have turned out for both of us, it seemed we had made some responsible decisions.

Our children would undoubtedly make their own mistakes, and we would be there for all of them whenever they needed us, just as Tom's parents had been.

After all, that's what it means to be family.

We made certain Grandpa Lugi came often and for extended stays so he could revel in the sweetness of all our grandbabies. We knew he was missing Tom's mother and loved on him as often as we could. He usually arrived January 2nd to escape the Cleveland gray winter days and would stay until the end of March.

His relationship with the children grew as they did. It was beautiful to watch him rolling on the floor with them as they wriggled and laughed.

I enjoyed his company each morning at the other end of the kitchen table. We sipped our coffee as he read the morning paper from cover to cover. I knew not to interrupt, so I answered emails and played games on my laptop until he moved from the table to the sofa for "Let's Make a Deal" and "The Price is Right." His critique of the contestants' answers as he watched the shows daily provided many humorous memories.

He felt loved and enjoyed the big dinners surrounded by family and friends.

Jude was a light in the darkness for the entire family. He would come to the house daily, so Lindsay could work at Wounded Warrior Project full time.

One day, he ran through the front door yelling, "Mia, Mia...," Lindsay and I looked at each other wondering what he was saying.

Mia? When he found me in the kitchen, he wrapped his arms around my legs and hugged me hard.

From that day forward I was known to Jude and eventually the rest of the family warmly as Mia.

I loved the new moniker. Since Matt's parents were his "Mimi and Poppy," Tommy and I had suddenly become "Mia and Poppa."

It was a beautiful name that reminded me of an Italian Nona and that seemed like another little God wink.

He arrived one Sunday for family dinner dressed in a green T-shirt that said, 'Big Brother."

Yes, we were having another baby scheduled to arrive in May just two years after Jude. We were elated. Jude had been such a beautiful gift during such a difficult time. We were thrilled to await another blessing.

Then, after two years of marriage, Louis and Emily announced they were expecting. Olive Adelle (her middle name lovingly honored Tom's mother) was born on January 1, 2016, a beautiful healthy baby girl.

The nursery upstairs was being put to good use. We now had eight grandchildren. We were grateful for healthy happy babies to fill our home.

62

Praying for Lung Cancer?

THE SUCCESSFUL NEW FOUNDATION TOOK up a great deal of my time, so the months seemed to pass quickly between each of my scans. Around my three-year Whipple-versary, my radial-oncologist noticed some spots in my lungs.

He described them as small ground-glass clusters that had no real form. He said they could be pre-cancerous, but we would continue to watch them.

The next few scans showed growth, and more were forming. He began to chart each one noting size and shape. While they were slow growing, it was troubling.

The natural progression of pancreas cancer is to move to liver, lungs, bones, or brain. As some of the spots took on form and reached a centimeter in size, he ordered a biopsy.

Dr. Ko felt this could be early-onset lung cancer. In fact, he hoped that was what it was.

"These spots are just not acting like pancreatic cancer," he said as he turned his head slightly.

"If they are lung cancer, we can treat this and hopefully stop the growth."

A painful needle biopsy was taken. However, the test was inconclusive.

My mind went back to the view of those two slides I had seen in the breakout sessions with the researchers in DC of breast cancer and pancreas cancer. I knew it would be difficult to capture, if any at all, of those nasty adenocarcinoma cells.

Ironically, we found ourselves praying it was lung cancer!

A cardiothoracic surgeon was brought into the loop, and we met with him in consultation prior to the biopsy.

"We will remove two or three wedges from your left lung where the largest spots are detected." Dr. Maki said. "Pathology will tell us what we are dealing with," he added.

The doctors agreed it was almost certainly lung cancer, best case scenario. Dr. Maki had suggested we wait six more months to see what happened to the tumors. But I felt a tug at my heart. Praying about what to do, as I had done when we faced each of the other decisions, I felt strongly we needed to find out what it was. The surgery needed to be performed now. He agreed and the operation was scheduled.

"Your lung will be deflated during surgery so the wedges can be removed," said Dr. Maki. "We will need to insert a drainage tube to remove any fluid that collects."

While this surgery was simple compared to the Whipple, I was filled with trepidation. The outcome from pathology could be dreadful if the PC had now metastasized to my lungs. I had to know what I was fighting.

Before I drifted out of consciousness on the operating table, Psalm 91 was once again my go-to. God was in command. I trusted Him with my life. Tommy and I prayed for His will and our acceptance of whatever outcome we would receive.

Three days' recovery in the hospital with the drainage tube was more painful than I had foreseen. Once the tube was removed, I felt immediate relief and home we went to await the report.

We left Mayo on a Friday, so we didn't expect to hear from anyone until Monday. It was a quiet weekend until Dr. Maki called and asked if Tommy was with me. He told us to put the phone on speaker so he could speak to both of us.

"I am completely surprised by this report," Dr. Maki said in a strange voice.

"The tumors are of pancreas cancer origin," he explained. "And, quite frankly, I am shocked."

Tommy became unhinged. "You all agreed it most probably would be lung cancer. How can this be?'

Dr. Maki had no explanation. "Tom, the slow formation and growth are not consistent with pancreas cancer."

We hung up the phone feeling deeply letdown.

"I'm calling Dr. Asbun," he said.

After a few minutes on the phone with my Whipple surgeon, a conference call was arranged with all the doctors.

Dr. Asbun recommended a second pathology be completed since the doctors concurred this was shocking news.

A few days passed and the second report concluded the same information. It had been confirmed. The pancreas cancer had moved into my lungs and treatment should be started soon.

A recurrence was always in the back of my mind. I had now become a statistic not customarily associated with PC. I had survived for over four years. And I was almost back to normal physically … well as normal as could be expected after a pancreaticoduodenectomy (Whipple resection). I knew I was fortunate to be a surgery candidate and to have the best surgeon and oncologists in the world. I was blessed beyond my expectations.

I was going to make a difference in this disease.

To my last breath.

63

"We Don't Have to Go Back."

Tommy and I love to travel to faraway places. Italy, Spain, Cancun, England, Paris, Las Vegas, California, New York City, Atlantis, Cleveland, Chicago. Most of the trips involved a casino situation. Tommy would plot ideas for the next trip before we had put our suitcases away.

Cancer didn't stop him.

Once the surgery and treatment were completed, we only had the scans to worry about. They would be scheduled every six to eight weeks in the beginning.

Tommy would announce a trip just as soon as the scan results came in. For three-plus years, the reports were stable. And his creativity was boundless. He would wave a trip in front of me like the starting flag at Daytona.

Then it happened. The spots in my lungs were not only growing, but they were also multiplying. Uncertainty once again soared to the surface. It was always there, just tucked away deep within. Was this the beginning of a downward spiral? Would those spots now grow out of control and consume the rest of my body?

A meeting with my oncologist was scheduled. We needed to return to chemotherapy treatment as soon as possible. Dr. Mody had a plan of treatment options. He felt oral chemotherapy, Capecitabine, was a good place to start.

A few days later the drug arrived via FedEx. It came with lots of instructions. Do not touch pills, flush twice, etc. It was strange to look at this large oval orange pill and think about the force it contained to eradicate potentially lethal cells.

My next scan was January 2019. The results proved Capecitabine to be ineffective for me. One of the spots had doubled in size. Dr. Mody said I needed to begin chemotherapy infusions immediately. This time Gemcitabine/Abraxane would be administered every two weeks.

A new building had been constructed on the Jacksonville Mayo campus to handle patients with cancer. The chemo suites were simple but spacious and appealing. Each held a smart TV with free movies. There was a small sofa for a visitor to sit. It was comfortable and private. Much different than the previous setup in the main building where you sat in a reclining chair surrounded by curtains that could be pulled for privacy from the other three or four patients.

Sometime around the third chemo infusion it started. The base of my hair hurt. It was a strange sensation. I knew something was different. My first chemo regimen I managed to avoid this startling side effect. But not this time. Maybe the addition of the Abraxane made the difference.

In the next few days my hair began to fall out in clumps, leaving long strands of silver white on my clothing. If I grabbed a hunk of hair, it would be left between my fingers.

I needed to think about a wig.

A trip to the beauty salon was in order. My amazing hair stylist had promised she would help. I was thankful for her. I made an appointment and Lindsay met me at the shop.

As the long white strands of hair fell to my cape like feathers floating from the sky, I experienced a huge sense of loss.

Lindsay silently grabbed my hand from beneath the cape, and I began to cry. My tower of strength, my angel. She was always at my side.

My platinum locks had always been my signature. Why does this beastly disease attempt to steal everything from you?

Much like Dr. Mody, I had my own arsenal in a God who walks beside me every step of the way. He guards me and He shelters me, and He saves me from the snares of battle. Cancer cannot take me. Only my Lord can take me home when He is ready.

I gathered my courage and said to myself, I'm going to make some fun of this. We were heading to the Lady Gaga concert in Vegas. She and Bradley Cooper had just released the smash hit "A Star is Born" and we couldn't wait to see her in person. The best wig shops had to be in Las Vegas!

This beast is not going to steal any more of my joy. After all, it is just hair. It will grow back. And, in the meantime, I will wear my baldness as a warrior wears a helmet, in the fight for my life.

God help me.

When the recurrence came in July 2018, we agreed to return to our happy place … Italy. Once again, the whole family would go.

Lindsay and Tom began to plan the details. This time we would travel to Capri and the Amalfi Coast, which we had never experienced. We would plan two days in Naples and a trip just twenty kilometers to Caserta, where Tom's great-grandfather had been born. Then, rent a villa in Sorrento and a boat to tour the cobalt Tyrrhenian Sea with its vibrant grottos and the umbrella-covered beaches of Capri and Positano.

It was a welcome diversion as we navigated our new reality.

The family together once again on an international excursion, laughing and singing and loving, just being together with no distractions. Everyone delighting in new sites, tastes, and smells. Enjoying what God had created and thankful for memories we would look back on to get us through the difficult days that lay ahead.

Tom and I relaxed on the bow of the boat, sipping Prosecco and watching as the kids swam in the icy waters of the Blue Grotto. The sounds of their laughter filled my head. He proposed a toast as we locked arms and clicked our plastic glasses.

"You don't have to go back, Mia, if you don't want to," he said lovingly. "We have enough to stay here for a while," he added.

"I could never leave the family," I responded with a smile.

"Well, that would make our stay a bit shorter," he laughed.

We looked into each other's eyes with such deep love at that moment. I knew he would give me anything my heart desired.

This is what true love looks like I thought. God had sent this unlikely character so many years before, to be my soulmate. What a sense of humor He has.

I was filled with gratitude for this and so many things, our life together, and the beautiful family that shared our blessings without restriction.

My Joseph, his Mary, it was biblical indeed.

We returned as planned and the chemo continued.

64

The Perfect Present

WHILE THE INFUSIONS BEGAN TO take a physical toll on me, I powered through as best I could. Days turned into weeks and weeks into months marked by the word "scan" on my calendar.

My body responded like a clock. I was filled with energy in the mornings and often make plans to prepare a meal or have everyone over for a swim in the evening. But, as the hours passed, I would get tired. My comfy bed would beckon me around three or four each day. I was physically spent.

Carmen would arrive each weekday afternoon with JTTF mail. She would walk slowly toward my bedroom door to see if I was asleep and check if I needed anything. She had become like a sister to me. We all loved how she greeted us with a full one-minute hug and shared how happy she was to see us. She loved the babies too. And they loved her.

My friends continued to love on me and lift me in prayer. I treasured the value of those relationships.

Many days Jude and Mick and little Olive would run through the front door questioning, "Are you in bed today, Mia?"

Most likely I was.

My Joseph had planned a trip to Atlantis in the Bahamas for our anniversary. Paradise Island was the destination of our honeymoon Viking Cruise thirty-six years ago. We had returned several times, but this time we were alone just as we were thirty-six years ago. Just a long weekend to relax in the sun and spend some time together.

It was extremely difficult to think of a favorable gift for my husband of over three decades. He was brutally honest as he opened his presents and lightheartedly suggested it was another failed attempt to please him.

He bought whatever he needed or wanted, so it was next to impossible to come up with anything at all … for not just me … all of us.

And yet, he was the best gift-giver ever. He would find the one thing you would love but would never buy for yourself. He just had a way about him. And presentation was everything.

One year, around the time I needed a new car, for Christmas, he went all out. As I opened the new pots and pans, the workout clothes, and the purses he had shopped for months, I would think I was done, but no.

Suddenly the music would blast, *Simply the Best* by Tina Turner, as he entered the family room with yet another wrapped present and a huge smile on his face.

"You didn't think you were done, did you?" he would beam.

The small box contained a set of keys.

I was escorted to the front door where the previously vacant driveway now held a bright yellow convertible with a huge red bow on the hood.

He made me cry tears of joy every Christmas. Well, every birthday, every anniversary, every so often. He was the best gift-giver ever … his love language, generous beyond your wildest dreams.

My friends would wait with anticipation to see what surprise awaited me on any celebration.

What could I give him that would even come close to something like that? It was an endless dilemma.

I had been working on my memoir for about four years, adding chapters and editing as I voyaged through this crazy time. Perhaps I could give him some chapters that detailed our falling in love. Yes, that was it. I would give him my recollection of our love story.

Printing out the pages I questioned how he would respond. Would he remember it as I had? Would he see this gift as anything more than the pages of paper it was printed on?

As we fastened our seatbelts on the flight to Paradise Island, I removed the folded pages from my carry-on and handed them to him.

"Happy Anniversary, Joseph," I said.

As the plane soared high into the Florida blue sky, he read the pages with great intent.

When he was finished, he folded them, and placed them carefully in his backpack without a word.

It wasn't until we had returned home that he shared my gift to him with some dear friends. I didn't know what he thought about and I was fearful of asking. I had worked for a long time, baring my soul. What did he think of my labor?

"Judi gave me the best gift she could ever have given me for our anniversary," he said. "She gave me our love story."

My heart was lifted as he shared with our friends how deeply he was touched by this gift.

Thank God!

Treatments were becoming more and more difficult, but I felt I had no choice other than to take the drugs that would fight off any further tumors and keep them all under control.

My seventieth birthday was approaching, and of course, Tommy was planning a fitting celebratory trip around my chemo and scan schedule.

He arranged with Dr. Mody for us to have a full week and a half to be away.

Then he called some friends. "Who wants to go to Napa?"

65

"Are You in Bed Today, Mia?"

IN THE GOLDEN HOUR WE sat with Pete and Pam at a small iron table under an umbrella sipping chilled white wine and noshing on scrumptious nibbles of cheese and dried meats. The vine-covered rolling hills are the perfect place to be as the sun sets on another fall day. We were grateful for the time spent in a heavenly space and happy to share our paradise with dear friends for their first visit to Napa.

The steroids I had been placed on gave me a puffy appearance, that "moon" face, but they also improved my energy level, and I drew on this as we strolled the chilly caves and steep hills of the vineyards.

Our days were relaxed with just two planned tours, lazy lunches, and dinners. It was fun to watch Pete and Pam discover this new world of wine and natural beauty along the Northern California coastline.

We loved spending time with these dear friends.

After ample days in Napa, we flew to Las Vegas to spend another few days at Caesar's Palace, taking in a show or two and spending countless hours at the slot machines, three-card poker tables, and lazy, scrumptious meals at our favorite restaurants.

By the time our trip ended, I was dreading my return to reality and chemotherapy.

"When I think about chemo, I taste and smell it," I confided to Tom on the plane from Sacramento to Vegas' McCarran Airport.

"I really am dreading it," I added.

He looked at me with sympathetic eyes but had no real solution to offer.

My niece Kathy who is head of nursing at a large Scottsdale hospital was planning on being in Orlando for a nursing symposium.

"How about I come visit for a few days before or after my Orlando trip ... if it's not too much?" she asked.

We don't get together often enough, so this visit was super special, and I looked forward to spending quality time just the two of us.

"I'll go with you to chemo and take care of you afterward," she added.

I was usually good for about two days after the infusion, and the third day the flu-like symptoms would hit me. I would spend the next few days on the sofa. I felt like I could handle the visit physically with no trouble.

Kathy made the drive from Orlando via Uber and arrived the morning after we got home from our trip. I was so happy to see her, and we spent the day catching up and visiting the children, some of whom she had never even met.

On Sunday we went to a Jags game and introduced her to our friends as we tailgated. She enjoyed the new experience and even more meeting our buddies.

During the game I wasn't feeling right and drank water instead of the usual wine or beer. Son Louis noticed it first.

"You okay, Momma?" he asked.

"Yes, I'm just a little jet-lagged maybe and not looking forward to chemo on Tuesday," I replied.

Monday, Kathy and I spent the day at the beach just relaxing and loving being together. She shared stories about her children and grandchildren and of course the scoop about how my sister Sherrie and her husband were doing.

I loved sharing with her how I had slowly discovered how God had worked in my life. Kathy listened intently as I revealed account after account of things that had occurred that had no conceivable explanation other than God. She agreed.

Kathy had accomplished so much in her life. I hoped she could see how God had woven the threads of her tapestry into a beautiful life of service and love for her family.

When Tuesday arrived, we headed to Mayo for bloodwork and an oncology appointment with Dr. Mody. My bloodwork proved to be fine, so a full dose of Gemcitabine/Abraxane was ordered. We made our way to the chemo floor.

I could smell the metallic taste of the chemo before I was hooked up as I sat in the chairs in the waiting room. I began to feel nauseous. Normally an anti-nausea drug was added to the chemo cocktail, plus a Neulasta patch would be applied to my arm to provide time-released anti-nausea medication. I just needed to tough it out.

Once home Kathy and I sat on the big sectional sofa. I grabbed a bed pillow and a warm blanket as I eased into a comfortable position. The meds had not seemed to halt the nausea.

Suddenly I became sick as I retched, and my head pounded.

What was happening? Kathy sprang into action grabbing a cool cloth to wipe my brow and help me back to the sofa.

After two days of continuous vomiting and no intake of food, Tommy and Kathy both suggested I go back to Mayo. Dr. Mody agreed to meet us in the ED. Kathy returned home to her family and job as I promised to keep her informed and was admitted into a regular room.

It was unclear what was going on. Bloodwork and several tests were completed while drugs were administered to stop the vomiting. I was placed in semi-isolation. Nurses entering my room were clothed in paper gowns and masks.

Five days in the hospital revealed I had a viral infection in my digestive system. The chemo had brought on this condition. I lost about ten pounds and was weak from not eating.

At home I struggled to regain my strength and worried about the "nauseas brought on by prolonged chemotherapy" Dr. Mody suggested before my hospital stay.

Chemo was scheduled for me in one week and I was still experiencing the nausea.

It appeared Dr. Mody thought it was all in my head.

The consultation room door opened and Dr. Mody entered with a smile.

"How are you feeling today?" he asked.

"I've made a decision," I said "I am not going to have chemo today. I want to take a break till after the holidays."

The bold decision to stop treatment was one I made prayerfully and on my own. I awaited his reaction.

Surprisingly it was positive. "Great," he said with a smile.

Every major decision I have made during this illness has been made prayerfully and with confidence that God is in control of my life. While the doctors practice science He gifted them with, He remains in control, not the doctors. And, my Joseph has respected each decision because he knows how I arrived at it.

This cancer that I now view as a blessing in our lives, has given us so many positive changes. It has brought our family closer to God, closer to one another. It empowered us to start a foundation to fund important research that will result in a simple test that could be administered to patients presenting with family history, predisposition, or early symptoms that have been dismissed in the past as other less serious digestive issues.

Every six to eight weeks I go to Mayo for scans and bloodwork to determine the status of my cancer. It is always a time of anxiety and concern as the date approaches. However, I have learned to listen to my body and believe that while I am feeling as good as I can, the cancer is still at bay.

The last three scans have been reported as stable. This means the thirteen spots in my lungs, while still clearly there and growing slowly are not at this moment out of control.

During this time, I have been strong and played with my babies, made some great meals for the family, sent the twins off to college, and loved on my Joseph. Each day making more and more memories.

I chose to carry on and take in each breath enjoying my family and friends in gratitude for the life we have been blessed with so abundantly until the day … the shoe drops.

66

Life Goes On

THE 2020 PLAYERS HAD RETURNED to March after several years being held in May. Tommy and I were looking forward to the week of festivities with great anticipation. His Dad was scheduled to come down and the family was geared up for a week of some of the best rounds in golf. Sometimes referred to as the fifth major tournament, we had always considered this one of our favorite weeks of the year.

In 2014, when I was diagnosed just a week before PLAYERS, it took on a somber mood in our backyard at least. But, six years later, I was still here and not just alive, but thriving. It was cause for celebration.

Plans for our fourth annual *Champions for Hope* event were well under way and our sponsors and friends were excited to get a look at what the TPC Stadium Course would hold for them just two and a half months later. And we were happy to entertain the participants around our outdoor bar for The PLAYERS tournament.

The week started off well with chamber of commerce weather, the reason the tournament had been moved to May to begin with. We had suffered through more than a few washouts over twenty-plus years. So, we wondered if moving the event back to March was a sound choice.

We planned to keep it low-key and limited to friends, sponsors of our event, and relatives and their guests. And this seemed to be working out beautifully.

Suddenly there was talk about an isolated disease that had stolen its way into the country from Wuhan, China. They were calling it Coronavirus, an infectious disease caused by severe acute respiratory syndrome, a form of SARS. We saw the images of mask and hazmat-clad Asians fighting this intruder that came to steal lives.

This highly contagious virus was suggested to be capable of a global pandemic with cases tracing back to November 2019 in China. Concerns for those with chronic diseases, immunocompromised people, and those over the age of 65 were considered high risk. The virus was spreading throughout Europe and Asia as rising numbers of cases and deaths were now being reported.

When the virus had reached the US shores, with active cases reported in Washington DC, New York, and California, the level of fear escalated; we were forced to face the dreadful possibilities.

An announcement came from PGA Tour Headquarters, The PLAYERS would be played; however, no spectators would be allowed on the course. This was unheard of but necessary to keep the players, volunteers, and fans safe amid the Covid-19 spread.

We gathered around the outdoor televisions to watch the most skilled golfers in the world compete for the title of PLAYERS Champion 2020 and the occasional breaking news story reporting on the virus.

Now the federal government took heed. Slow at first to respond to the worldwide outbreak, it was no longer possible to ignore. President Trump brought together the world's top disease control experts and heads of corporations to consider next steps. And they began to take action.

Governor DeSantis appeared on television to report the first cases in Florida and necessary mitigation steps needed to be taken to slow spread of the now deadly virus. He explained the new term "social distancing" to remain self-quarantined to avoid contact with others through handshakes and hugs. We were told to not touch our faces and to wash our hands frequently.

Thursday, late afternoon, Jay Monahan, Commission of Golf for the PGA Tour, made another announcement that shook us to our core. The 2020 Players was cancelled at the end of play of the first round.

This would be the first of an onslaught of cancelled events, the shutting down of the airlines, and eventually our borders. We managed to get Dad back up to Cleveland before the airlines shut down so he was safe in his own condo and around his daughters who would be sure he was doing well, eating, and healthy.

It wasn't long before it became obvious, we needed to cancel our fourth Champions for Hope Celebrity Golf event scheduled the first week of June. My eyes filled with tears as I wrote an email to our sponsors, board members, and volunteers: "For the safety of everyone, we were not holding the event this year."

We retreated to our homes and only went out occasionally for a drive in the car for a change of scenery. Tom would grab needed grocery items, so I didn't need to go to the grocery store.

Church was cancelled for the first time ever. It seemed as if the world was completely shut down.

Everything was cancelled and we were encouraged to stay in our homes quarantined. If you needed groceries, you could go to the store wearing a mask and following the rules of social distancing and in some cases one-way isles were marked. Ten-inch pieces of tape marked off each six-foot interval in the checkout lanes. It was surreal.

Life would never return to normal.

67

The Pandemic

2020

S O MANY THEORIES SURROUNDED THE Covid-19 virus pandemic. Some believed conspiracy schemes had been concocted to undermine rightwing conservatives. There was an election approaching. But this was global. And our President, in three and a half short years, had turned the world upside down. While the Republicans who supported him saw his campaign promises come to fruition, trade sanctions resulting in more jobs and a strong economy, border walls secured, and much more, he had made many enemies amongst world leaders and democrats who continued to feed the media with criticism, leading to extreme divides as he tweeted relentlessly in his defense.

Then came the shutdowns. Schools, churches, events, any function where more than ten people gathered.

As the case numbers increased and the death tolls were announced, I knew regardless, I could not take a chance. So, I sheltered in place and looked forward to the visits of my family and the little ones who were also sheltering. They would come for a dip in the pool and a change of scenery.

Each morning I read and watched the news with trepidation, not certain if I should believe what was reported and, becoming desensitized by the reports of refrigerated semi's housing dead coronavirus fatalities, accounts of tearful doctors and nurses physically and emotionally drained caring for Covid-positive patients on ventilators and in the ED and ICU's.

While I feared getting Covid, I was already facing death. Turning on the television just upset me. I didn't need to have any more stress on my body.

Was it the end times? I began to join Fr. Matt live stream as he said the afternoon prayers. I had not missed mass until now. I longed for the Eucharist and the fellowship of seeing our church family each Sunday.

When church finally did open, it was required that we sign up and only half of the church would be seated. You had to have a ticket and a mask to enter. If you were over sixty-five or if you had underlying medical issues, you were asked to shelter at home, leaving me out.

Nothing in my lifetime had ever shut down a country ... our country, the most powerful country in the free world. The skeptic in me continued to question the numbers. The winter flu had historically and unfortunately caused deaths. The numbers for coronavirus globally were not even near the flu numbers. But the speed with which it spread was alarming. Unlike influenza, there was no vaccine to stop it or even control it. But reports assured us several companies were working tirelessly on a vaccine.

The eternal optimist, I looked for the silver lining and strangely saw it clearly emerge from the panic surrounding us. The pandemic had brought families together, parents and students working virtually from home, thrust together for better or for worse. The proverbial hamster wheel had stopped for an undetermined amount of time. No more church services, school, no more sports, no bars or restaurants were open, no weddings, gatherings of more than six people were discouraged. While it was disturbing, part of me knew something had to change to unite our families once more. We had reestablished what the family unit resembled; however, it was nowhere close to biblical.

The pandemic had forced us all to reconnect, to share in the responsibility once more of teaching our children and seeking ways to entertain ourselves. Puzzle and board game boxes were brought down from the closet shelf and dusted off. Families were joining together in the kitchen to prepare a meal. They were having meaningful conversations.

Of course, the painful downsides emerged along with the good. Small businesses failed under the closures. Unemployment skyrocketed as families looked to the government to help them put food on the table. Mental health issues of depression, suicide, drug abuse, and domestic violence brought on by isolation shot up. Nursing homes and hospitals could not allow visitors for our most susceptible population in concern of the spread of the virus. Many died alone or in the presence of brave and exhausted healthcare workers but separated from their loved ones.

There had been no global pandemic of this proportion for one hundred eighteen years.

And then it happened … May 25th, 2020, a forty-six-year-old Black man was killed in Minneapolis, Minnesota by the police as they were attempting to arrest him for allegedly using a fake counterfeit bill. They pinned him to the ground with a knee to his neck, cutting off his breathing. He kept telling them he couldn't breathe, but the police never let him up. He tried to call out for his Momma. It was horrific.

As the months slowly passed, violence emerged. The over two hundred years of oppression and inequality surfaced in acts of extreme hostility, race against race, gender, ethnicity, government authority, and social or economic position. There was a rumbling that could no longer be contained.

Black Lives Matter became the mantra. No longer could repression be ignored, swept under the rug, or accepted. It was well past time for change. Much needed transformation in our core beliefs to unify the nation that had been built on a reported false foundation of trust in God, freedom, and acceptance of anyone who landed on our shores.

Peaceful protests quickly turned violent as businesses were looted and burned. Statues glorifying those who were a part of our nation's history, who had created this oppression, were pillaged and pulled down.

Large cities could no longer control the violence and some really didn't care to try. It was at a point where protests seeded by police brutality against Blacks reached a boiling point. The silent majority retreated even further, afraid they would not be seen as politically correct by the protesters no matter what they said or believed.

I turned off the TV; I just couldn't bear to watch it. I prayed for God to return soon.

And somewhere God looked down, I am sure with tears in His eyes.

68

Love

GOD IS GOD AND DOES not take sides. He is for all of us. The diversity that we beckoned to build this nation was now dividing us, ripping us apart.

It seemed overwhelming and impossible to fix. Yet, it was so simple. That one four-letter word that is repeated in the Bible KJV three hundred and ten times. If we could all just show love. The kind of love Jesus showed. That agape love that is unconditional. The love we all seek in our own lives. And love is free if we are willing to accept and give it.

But it was not going to happen overnight. Generations of prejudice had sustained the belief that the color of our skin or the number of vowels in our name made us different. Hearts needed softening, minds needed opening, only faith could be the conduit for the colossal change that needed to be made. All of this had to be replaced with love.

Yes, we needed a miracle.

But, as we have seen, our God is a God of miracles. I saw it in my own life. Now I needed to see it wash over the world like a tsunami.

Wash away the hatred and the prejudice. Replace it with seeds of love, acceptance, and unity.

As of this writing, we sit amid it all, perhaps the eye of the storm. If I were a betting person, I would bet God will once again show His mighty hand. I believe with my entire being He will not allow Satan to win. And so, I pray He will return soon.

If you are gripped in fear for any reason, physical abuse, a cancer diagnosis, a global pandemic, or oppression that seems it will never erase from your life, seek God's protection. Refuge lies just under His wing feathers as He promises in Psalm 91. He will fight your battles for you.

Ephesians 6:17: *And take the helmet of salvation and the sword of the Spirit, which is the word of God.*

In the book of Revelation 16:15: *Take note, I will come as unexpectedly as a thief!*

And in 1 Thessalonians 5; 1-10 Paul writes to his people that God will return to earth again:

For, we know the day of the Lord will come unexpectedly.

Behold I stand at the door and knock, it says in Revelation 3:20, *if anyone hears my voice and opens the door, I will come.*

You only need to pray for Him to come into your heart to be assured of eternity in heaven, free from all pain and sorrow and suffering.

Your personal story is filled with miracles you might have never noticed. It took me many years to see the hand of God in my own life. It is my sincere hope you will discover Him and thank Him for all He has done.

And, when the day comes when we face Him, I pray our robes will glisten with gold and silver threads and make us worthy to sit at His feet as He shares the answers to all our questions.

69

A Little Slice of Heaven

Fall 2022

F OR SEVERAL YEARS, MY JOSEPH and I searched around Asheville, NC, for a mountain house we could leave to the children as a legacy property. In January of 2021, we found the perfect spot, a thirty-three-acre farm just outside the city and about ten minutes from the AVL airport.

Had you told me, a few years before that my Cleveland born and raised city boy would even give a farm a second thought, I would have said you were crazy. But we found the farm including a large main house, workshop with an apartment on top, pole barn, log cabin, barn, seven pastures, and an orchard that ends along state-stocked Cane Creek, then reaches five acres up beautiful Berny Mountain. Plenty of room and accommodations for our ever-growing family.

Tommy happened upon the property online and sent me a video with one question. "Would you ever consider a farm?"

We visited the property mid-January and fell in love even though there was not one leaf on a tree, the winter view. It promised so much for the children to do. Fishing in the rocky creek, campfires, picking apples and peaches from the orchard, and then the possibility of farm animals made us fall in love with this gem instantly.

We closed late March and began to restore the farm to even greater than its original beauty. We had a goal of furnishing, painting, and readying the place for a family unveiling the weekend of July 4th.

Thirteen mattresses were ordered online as we happened upon a great rustic Amish furniture store where we were able to completely furnish the houses in a style consistent with this mountain retreat.

My sweet brother and nephew helped us getting gas, electric, water up and running as they freshly painted the walls and prepared the chicken coop and goat pen for our new pets. Each day brought a new challenge to this farm that had been basically vacant for about two years.

It was such fun putting everything together, shopping and working hard to reach our goal of completion by the time the family would arrive. And we were able to accomplish just that.

A year and a half later, as I sit here in main house, I recall the day I asked Tommy if it was real or were we already in heaven. We have had many visits of family and friends who all describe it as a very spiritual place, such a drastic change from our home near the beaches of Florida.

We are getting used to farm life with animals who give us great joy but anchor us in the fact that chickens get eaten by hawks and sheep die from pneumonia, donkeys and goats need their hoofs trimmed periodically. There is nothing more beautiful than three cows and a rescue horse in the lush green pastures on the property.

The donkeys, who live to be as old as forty, were named after the two characters in the family most associated with jackasses ... Lou and

Dom! They are my favorites, the donkeys and both or their namesakes. The animals are named after family members living and deceased. It was simple to tag the place with the name ... *Z Family Farm.*

The darkhaired fainting goats, not quite a year old, are growing quickly. Today I noticed their coats were growing longer and thicker as were the wooly white Dorper sheep with their dark black heads. Just two months before the sheep had been shorn and just like that, they resembled curly, plump pin cushions. Fall is approaching and God is preparing our animals for cold winds and winter snows. I have witnessed the complete weather cycle, and it reminds me how quickly the seasons change in the southern mid-west after living in Florida for over fifty years.

We asked Fr. Matt if he would consider visiting our farm and blessing the property and the animals. He agreed enthusiastically. His trip was special, and along with some dear friends, we witnessed him sprinkle holy water on the animals and say prayers over the cornfield and pasture land as well as the houses and barns, asking God to bless all those who visited and to keep this place a haven for those who visit to experience His peace that surpasses all understanding.

I am sure God has sent us a little glimpse of what it is like in heaven at His beautiful creation that transforms each season gifting us with flowers, greenery, lush grasses, fruits and vegetables, birds, and even flaming leaves and fireflies. Oh, and nine acres of corn!

Tommy and I are deeply grateful for the blessing of this special place where we can escape the heat and enjoy our time with family and friends.

We rest in the fact the family will enjoy this beautiful haven for generations to come.

The cancer has returned. We are thankful for God's continued grace with immunotherapy treatments that have little side effects and will possibly give me more time. And while I can, I will enjoy each moment and make the most of it.

Now, again, our friends, family and even people we have yet to meet pray for us. This gift is one that is free and easy. The rewards are beyond our imagination.

And you be assured, in return, we pray for all the families who pray for us.

We are forever blessed and thankful for your love and support.

May God's blessings be upon you all the days of your life.

Epilogue

Thank You for Your Love and Prayers.

June 2022

"For you created my inmost being, you knit me together in my mother's womb. I praise you because I am fearfully and wonderfully made; your works are wonderful … Your eyes saw my unformed body; all the days ordained for me were written in your book before one of them came to be."—Psalm 139:13-14a,16 (NIV)

THE CANCER HAS RETURNED, REPORTED Dr. Babiker. "There are spots on your liver we are concerned about, a lymph node near your pancreas that is lit up and a tumor in the reconstructed part of your pancreas. The lung tumors are growing."

"How much time do we have, doctor? Tom's voice quivered as he spoke.

"I am not God," Dr. Babiker answered. "However, without treatment, three to six months."

We pray for God to once again give us the wisdom to choose the right path, the treatment that will give me quality of life and maybe even another miracle of remission. We never pray for healing, we pray for the strength and courage to accept His will, whatever that may be. Thankful for the incredible time He granted us to see five grandbabies come into the world, weddings, trips, Grandpa's healing, love of my sweet husband growing every moment since we began this cancer journey.

But, most importantly, to see the faith of our family and our friends grow beyond our imagination. What gifts He has showered us with. The prayers of our friends for our family will never be forgotten. The kindnesses of dinners, flowers, cards, and texts mean so much and brighten even the darkest days. Our gratitude cannot be measured or expressed.

I can rest in the knowledge that my family believes ... my friends believe, and we can weather any storm, any trial because we know that in the end, we will all be together in heaven for all of eternity.

Life never ends, it just transforms. We will always be together, so long as we know Jesus. And best of all we have lived our earthly lives learning and refining our hearts in His image, just as He instructed, preparing to be even the least bit worthy to sit at His feet.

So, as I end this story of the weaving of my tapestry, ragged and torn yet sparkling with the jewels of His crown and the rich colors of the joyous miracles He has granted, I pray you seek Him and be blessed when you learn the magic of His mysteries and graces.

You too can share in this wonderful weaving of your life's story.

I know it will be beautiful!